the
Ecosystem Pond

From the Publisher of Aquascape Lifestyles Magazine

AQUASCAPE
LIFESTYLES
BOOKS

photo by Bill Richert

Publisher & Editor In Chief
Greg Wittstock

Managing Editor
Tamara Hughes

Senior Staff Writer
Kelly Tunney Clancy

Editor At Large
Rick Osbourne

Graphic Design Service
Icon Digital Design & Illustration, Inc.

Creative Director
Michael P. Stout

Senior Art Director
Rick Byers

Art Directors
Colleen Haveman
Dan Lohmann

The Ecosystem Pond
ISBN #0-9753123-0-8
is published by
The Pond Guy Publications™,
a division of Aquascape Designs, Inc.®,
P.O. Box 638, West Chicago, IL 60186
www.aquascapedesigns.com

Cover photo by Wemco Landscapes

AQUASCAPE
LIFESTYLES
BOOKS

the Ecosystem Pond

*Creating, Caring for and Loving
Your Own Backyard Water Garden*

Contents

Chapter 1

The Meaning of Water Gardens

How Deep Does It Really Go?

by Greg Wittstock

Water gardening is hot! Many people are spending lots of money to install picturesque ponds, babbling brooks, cascading waterfalls, colorful fish, and beautiful aquatic and terrestrial foliage in a vast variety to create one-of-a-kind, living, breathing backyard paradises.

Americans are finally learning to stop and smell the roses, especially the ones that are growing close to home. We're learning to appreciate the things we have, the things we used to take for granted. We're trying to make the most out of every day, every week, and every month.

photo by Scott Hughes

The Passion of Water Gardening

This phenomenon even has a name. It's called cocooning— — the appreciation of things close to home. By all accounts, it has a lot to do with the healthy state of the water gardening industry today. But the economy is the economy, and numbers are only numbers, and neither one can really explain the passionate depth of feeling that many water gardeners experience when it comes to their ponds.

If I've heard one water gardener, I've heard 50 who say, "Now that I have a pond I would never live in a house without one again." Or, "Now everything revolves around the pond. Breakfast, lunch, dinner, entertainment, even kid-raising is made easier with a beautiful, naturally balanced, aquatic eco-system, sitting in the backyard."

The Perfect Family Entertainment

It's amazing how many kids don't care as much about television or video and computer games when a great water garden is within a stone's throw. They'd rather be out checking the fish, frogs, turtles, and anything else they can find. The water garden is a natural antidote to the electronic addictions that have infected so many kids in this modern technological age. Family entertainment and environmental education take place next to the water garden.

Father-Son Bonding

For Mike Kurylo of Germantown, Maryland, having a pond proved to be a common language and a common interest that

Mike Kurylo and his father, enjoying their mutual hobby of pondering.

overshadowed the many differences he had with his father. "Dad got his pond in 1995 and I helped put it in. I got mine in 1998 and I helped install that one too.

"Ever since the ponds came into our lives, it's given my dad and I something in common, something to talk about that just wasn't there before," Mike said. In the spring, Mike and his dad do their spring pond cleanouts together and then they make the trek to the local nursery to buy plants. "We've purchased fish together and we swap experiences. Whenever I have a pond problem to solve, I always ask his advice, and whenever he runs into something that he's never seen before, he calls and asks me what I know about it too," Mike added. When they get together to talk, it's always out by the pond, weather permitting, of course.

Tom and Dolly Horan relaxing by their pond.

In Memory Of ...

Tony Sargeant is a professional pond installer from Sharpsburg, Georgia who built a pond for his parents 10 weeks before his father passed away. As a result, the pond carries a very special meaning for Tony and his family.

"Dad was a guy who worked hard all his life and never had a lot to show for it," Tony said. "He hunted and went fishing when he could find the time, but he never did think he could afford to have something nice like a backyard pond." Tony's dad was so proud of his pond, and so proud of the fact that his son had installed it for him. His dad passed away at age 64, only two years into retirement, and he was never able to afford what some folks might call nice things. This pond changed all that.

"Mom still calls it Dad's pond and says that when Dad was home he was always out on the front porch checking out the fish and plants, and generally enjoying life in a way that he was unable to before the pond," Tony said. "Mom says that if he'd had it for only one day, from the look in his eyes, it was worth the time and effort."

Simplicity

Tom Horan, a pond enthusiast from Arlington Heights, Illinois said, "At the heart of my own water gardening is a sense of simplicity. In the 21st century, everything has become so fast paced, so high tech, so incredibly complicated, that it's hard to slow down, it's hard to simplify life, even when you know it's in need of simplification."

So when Tom and his wife, Dolly, sit out by the pond with a hot cup of coffee and the morning paper in hand, they feel like the world slows down just a bit. "I'm back in control in a way that I never am when I'm out on the four-lane, or when I'm trying to stay on top of things at the office," Tom said. "But when I sit down out by the pond, kick my feet up on the coffee table, and let the soothing sounds of the waterfall soak clear into my bones, life is richer, more enjoyable, and yes, it's simpler."

Geographical and Social Center of the House

"I'm kind of a real estate-oriented person," Dolly Horan said. "And I see the pond as the most important room in our house. It's where we take most

"The pond is my sanity, and nothing less, I swear it is," pond owner Frank Stompanato says with a grin.

Matt and Laurie Nicholson expect to spend a lot of time at home, enjoying their backyard with their new family.

of our meals, it's where we entertain, and it's where we go to catch a breath and relax at the end of a tough day."

For many people these days, the television set is the thing the family congregates around. For others, it's the computer or video games. But for the Horan family, it's the pond that attracts. "It's the whole experience, from the soothing sounds of the waterfall, to the aroma of the prolific plants. We just love to spend our time around the pond," Dolly said.

Youth and Playfulness

Along a similar line, Matt Nicholson says that his pond transports him back to his youth, to a little town in Michigan, close to Lake Huron. "I spent so much time in and around the water. I mean, when I sit beside the pond, I feel like Tom Sawyer or Huck Finn sneaking back into the woods along the Mississippi River or one of those Norman Rockwell kids swinging out over the local watering hole on a tire swing. That's how I feel when I'm sitting out by the pond," Matt said.

A Family Affair

"For me it's a family thing," Pilar Stompanato of Bartlett, Illinois, said. "It seems to bring people together, to put everyone in a relaxed state of mind, and to promote a good, old-fashioned, uninterrupted give and take among people who are sitting around the pond."

There's just something about the pond that helps people let their hair down. "It always feels to me like there is less facade, less ego, less 'putting on' when you're out by the pond," she added. Parents get to know their kids better when they're not being distracted by MTV or the latest video game. And when friends come over, they share colorful thoughts and ideas that really count, instead of extrinsic things like what kind of car you drive or what neighborhood you live in. "I guess I love what the pond does to bring people together," Pilar said.

An Organic Stress Reliever

For Frank Stompanato, Pilar's husband, the pond is an organic stress reliever, a diversion from the stress and strains of the modern-day world. "When I get in the car in the morning and head to work, it's bumper to bumper frustration. When I get to the office it's one project on top of another," Frank said.

When Frank heads home and pulls into the driveway, he's ready to escape from the work-a-day world. Before the pond came along, Frank would go straight to the television to unwind from the day. Today, he goes straight to the pond, kicks off his shoes, feeds the fish and lets the rhythm of the waterfalls make him human again. "The pond is my sanity, and nothing less, I swear it is," Frank laughed.

One Final Note

Water falling into a stream, meandering down into a pond sounds tranquil, peaceful, and decompresses the most stressed out mind. It's also a neighborhood attraction that creates friends out of neighbors that you never knew existed. It turns fish into finger-sucking pets, and at night, with the under-water lights on display, there's no way to overestimate the moonlit pond's ability to transform an ordinary evening into an extraordinary evening.

In the end, a pond means different things to different people. But, if you read between the lines and dive beneath the surface, what you'll find is more than a little bit interesting. So, go ahead and see how deep the meaning of ponds can really be. If you do, you won't be disappointed.

Chapter 2

Water Gardening Through the Ages

A Historical Look at Water's Role in the Garden

by Jennifer McGowan

For decorative or practical use, water features have been part of our landscape since the beginning of recorded history. From the simple water basins of ancient Persian gardens, to the elaborate water jets of the Renaissance Period, water gardening has taken on many forms through the ages. Some civilizations incorporated the cultivation of aquatic plants, while others focused solely on the mechanics of water transport and its ornamental uses in the garden. Today's backyard ponds reflect centuries of cultural influences and technological advances.

Taking a practical approach to water garden design, early ponderers built water features with steps and ledges that gave them access to the water as the level dropped from evaporation. Standing on a ledge, gardeners dipped buckets into the lower levels so they could give their plants a daily

watering. The shelves also allowed them to grow marginals, or plants that thrive in shallow water. Lilies, lotus, and reeds grew in the private ponds of Egypt, and many of these plants were used to craft baskets and writing instruments.

When in Rome, Garden As the Romans Do

Romans used water in their private residences for drinking, bathing, and irrigation. To reduce the evaporation that occurred in the process of transporting water to the home, the Romans developed qanats, or sheltered canals. These qanats were used the same way that we use rubber tubing in our fountains and water features, connecting water sources with their intended destinations. When the aqueducts were built, they gained greater control over water pressure and speed.

The Romans constructed fountains, thereby combining water pressure and garden art. Roman gardens tended to revolve around, and to feature, their engineering prowess and their love of sculpture, in contrast to the Egyptian's naturalistic focus on aquatic plants and fish.

Ponding in Paradise

Cyrus the Younger of Persia, a descendant of Cyrus the Great, named his garden Pairidaeza, a combination of the words "around" and "wall." Pairidaeza translates into our word for paradise and it was in the gardens of Persia that the concept of a garden escape was born.

Water was essential to the Pairidaeza garden. It physically outlined and divided the walled planting beds into sections, and symbolized the presence of life. Water storage containers, such as tubs and basins, which were kept in the garden symbolized abundance.

As in Rome, the Persians also used qanats to transport water. They constructed filtration screens called chadars, and used fountain jets for aeration and insect control. These two early devices are the precursors to the filters and pumps that are in use today. Upon arriving in the garden, water separated it into four equal plots. The channels of water met in the center of the garden, in a small pool or rectangular basin. The symmetrical layout of these gardens can be seen today in the design of Persian rugs.

Arabian Nights, Arabian Ponds

After conquering the Persian Empire, the Arab people modified water gardening slightly by adopting the concept of Pairidaeza while exalting water's importance. Constantly searching for new water sources in the desert made the Arabs revere water, and they, in turn, made it the dominant feature in their gardens. They transported water from springs, rivers, and lakes into storage tanks which, when full, would flow into a series of channels that irrigated the garden.

The need for garden irrigation was combined with the cooling principles of water evaporation, so open channels ran all through the garden to cool the surrounding air as the water evaporated. Garden fountains were not a prominent feature, but when present, they were conservative and quiet, in keeping with the respect for water.

Today's backyard ponds reflect centuries of cultural influences and technological advances.

Asian Interpretations

The driving force in early Asian garden design was the imitation of nature. Ponds and flowing water in natural settings were scaled down and recreated in private gardens. Courtyard gardens in Japan often featured simple fountains and pools. Wealthy families created

large ponds containing islands and sandy shorelines that looked like small ocean scenes. These "mock seas" were usually large enough for boating and fishing. Families used these man-made water features as a place to gather, reflect, and perform rituals and ceremonies.

At the beginning of the 10th century, Buddhism began to sweep Japan and the pond was used as a focal point in most gardens. With the rise in popularity of Zen Buddhism in the 14th century, water gardening was interpreted in the Zen fashion. Water features were replaced with beds of white sand that were painstakingly raked in straight lines and circles, to represent still and flowing waters.

Ponding Like an Egyptian

Some of the first "ponders" hailed from the deserts of Egypt, where the oldest surviving garden plan, dating back to 1400 BC, was discovered. The first known civilization to have designed and cultivated formal water gardens, Egyptians placed tremendous importance on moving and storing their water both practically and decoratively.

Water flowed to the private residences of Egypt through canals for domestic and irrigation use. The Egyptians made the most of water's presence in the garden by building ornamental ponds that were usually rectangular or T-shaped. Providing the focal point of most gardens, these ponds were used for festivities, ceremonies, and rituals. Almost all temples had water features for this purpose, the largest of which is the Sacred Lake at Karnak. Tomb paintings show fish in the water garden, which Egyptians bred to supplement their diet. They also used the "fishy" water as fertilizer. The pools had to be emptied and cleaned regularly, as filtration systems hadn't been developed yet.

Try to think of a well-known garden in history that hasn't contained a water feature, whether natural or man-made.

The Popularity of Koi

The beginning of the 17th century saw the return of the pond to the Japanese garden. Also, there was a rise in popularity of koi breeding when rice farmers kept koi in their ponds to provide a protein supplement for their diet. First recorded in written history in the middle of the 3rd century in China, koi were described as having red, white, black, and blue colorations. Little written history exists about the presence of koi in the garden between the 3rd and 17th centuries, but the hobby became popular in Japan in the early 1900's and later caught on in the Western world in the mid-1950's.

Renaissance Takes Water to Excess

Renaissance period gardens showcased water in a big way. Italian gardens such as Villa d'Este featured outrageous fountains, waterfalls, cascades, water steps, spouts, and water tables. The Italians emulated the Roman gardeners and their passion for fountains, symmetry, and proportion and focused on moving water in the garden, to the near exclusion of aquatic plants.

Formal Gardens and Grand Estates

Excess was a design concept in 17th century France. Courtyards were embellished with fountains and symmetrical pools bordered by shrubs and formal beds such as those at Versailles. The gardens and residences were planned together to maintain continuity in design. The fantastic fountains and water jets of the period were designed to complement and highlight the grand estates. Long, straight lines, massive structures, and high maintenance were prominent themes in the water features of this time.

In the 17th and 18th centuries, the English shed excess and brought Asian influences to the garden by emphasizing

untamed nature. This new movement in gardening went by the names Romantic, Picturesque, and Pastoral. Symmetry and geometric shapes were replaced by meandering rivers and irregularly shaped ponds surrounded by informal mass plantings. The goal was to achieve a look that bordered on being unkempt and wild.

New Country, New Water Features

The cultural melting pot of early America was apparent in the varied styles of its early gardens. Spanish settlers in the southwest built farmsteads and missions in the Roman tradition, with walled gardens featuring wellheads and fountains in the center. Designed to be both functional and decorative, these fixtures served as a water source for the garden while creating

used for fishing, boating, or relaxing. Water features of this period were very low key, as the emphasis was on mirroring the natural landscape.

The Victorian Period saw a brief return to formal manicured gardens. The cultivation of lilies and other water plants that could be kept in conservatories also became popular as increased travel led to the discovery and importation of exotic water plants. This trend continued to increase well into the mid-20th century when people began investing in home and landscape improvement.

The trend still continues today. Everything centers around the home — enjoying it, improving it, and even trying to run businesses from it. Water gardening increases the pleasure we get from our surroundings and adds value to the land we own. Improved technology has made water gardening a highly accessible and affordable hobby that is open to the many personal tastes and cultures that make up our country. Try to think of a well-known garden in history that hasn't contained a water feature, whether natural or man-made. It's clear that water in the garden is here to stay. ✎

a peaceful setting. English settlers in hot and humid towns like Charleston, and French settlers in New Orleans, also placed fountains in the middle of their garden courtyards to create cool resting spots.

The influence of the Picturesque movement was evident in the sprawling plantations of the South and in the manors of the North. These large properties usually had a pond that was

Chapter 3

The 20 Most Problematic Myths

Understanding the Facts Helps Avoid Headaches!

L ike any other culture in the world, the pondering culture has its own mythology which has grown and matured over the years. However, just because our ancestors always thought it was true, doesn't necessarily make it true. Here, 20 "old-wives tales" are examined and the facts set straight … once and for all.

1) Predators will eat all of your fish!

There is a constant fear in the water gardening community that raccoons and other four-legged predators will go swimming in your pond, and while they're in there, they'll help themselves to some of your prize koi, shubunkin, or goldfish.

You'll find that having rocks and gravel in your pond not only makes it look better, but it makes it healthier as well.

When you go out to your pond in the morning and discover you're missing a fish or two, it's very tempting to blame it on such critters, especially if you didn't see it happen. There has to be a reasonable explanation, and predators are as good as any, right?

However, take the following facts into consideration before you jump to any conclusions. Raccoons generally won't swim. That's not to say they never swim, or couldn't stand on the side of your pond late at night and take a paw swipe or two at fish who are touring their way around the edge of your pond. Fortunately, most fish will swim to a deeper, more protected part of the pond when a predator is threatening them.

Muskrats, on the other hand, can swim and they do eat fish. Their presence is uncommon, and they're usually only found around water features that are close to larger bodies of water, like a retaining pond or a lake.

The one predator with legitimate credentials is the blue heron. These tall, long-legged, big-beaked birds can easily wade into your pond and help themselves to any fish they think look

tasty, and fly away with their belly full. They are a protected species, so they are off-limits if you're thinking about taking revenge on them. However, a scarecrow, a motion-sensing sprinkler that can be set up alongside your pond, ready to fire a steady stream of water at a heron, has had some degree of success in warding off these curious critters. It's a good idea to move the sprinkler often though, to keep them guessing.

Giving your fish a place to hide dramatically helps their odds of survival. Plenty of lily pads give them some protection and will work to minimize attracting a heron in the first place. Other protection measures include a cave-like structure that can be built in during the pond's excavation, or, if you already have a pond, they can be added with a little pond remodeling.

Rocks are essential in creating these hiding places in your pond. Crevices, or miniature caves, can be created within the rock walls of your pond. If you have the space, or have larger fish to accommodate,

Heron are territorial and can be scared away by a decoy.

You can use a 6-inch drain tile or PVC pipe to create even larger

You can place the PVC pipe right next to an existing shelf and hide it with some flat rocks.

down the fish waste and debris that would otherwise accumulate in the pond and turn into sludge. Regardless of your pond's location (i.e. close to trees and loads of leaves), or how many fish you have in it, you'll find that having rocks and gravel in your pond not only makes it look better, but it makes it healthier as well.

So contrary to the myth, having rocks and gravel on the bottom of your pond

Supplemental bacteria helps break down fish waste and debris.

you can use a 6-inch drain tile or PVC pipe to create even larger caves. Simply dig out a portion of one of the shelves and place the tile accordingly. You can then disguise the PVC with rock and gravel to blend it into your pond.

If your pond is already constructed, you can place the same drain pipe right next to an existing shelf and hide it with some flat rocks. Either of these options will allow your fish to find shelter and protection whenever any predator threat occurs.

The possibility of pond predators seeking out your pond is, indeed, a valid concern in terms of the safety of your pond's inhabitants, but the possibility shouldn't be a reason to avoid building a pond.

2) The presence of rocks and gravel makes it difficult to clean your pond.

You are susceptible to buying into this myth *if, and only if, you've never experienced pondering with rocks and gravel in your pond.* If you have a smooth-bottom pond, and each season you're amazed at the

amount of muck and grime that collects on the bottom, you automatically rule out rocks as a solution. You keep visualizing that same amount of muck on top of the rocks and gravel … and say, "NO!" to even considering them. It's understandable. It seems logical … until you learn the rest of the story.

Rocks and gravel offer a natural place for aerobic bacteria to colonize and set up housekeeping. This bacteria breaks

actually allows Mother Nature to clean up after herself, saving you headaches and hours of work trying to keep the bottom of your pond muck-free.

photo by Richard Witkiewicz

3) UV lights such as those in the UltraKlear™ UVC are the best way to keep your pond water clear.

UV clarifiers are indeed one way to keep your pond water clear, but certainly not the only way, and arguably not the natural way. The fact of the matter is that if you have a pond that's naturally balanced, in which the aquatic circle of life is rotating the way that Mother Nature intended, you don't need UVC at all. In this naturalistic setting, the fish eat the plants, then they produce the waste, which gets broken down (along with other pond debris) by aerobic bacteria that's colonized on the rocks and gravel below, and then it's taken back up as nutrition by the plants … round and round, forever and ever. A naturally balanced pond is a low maintenance pond because Mother Nature is doing the maintenance work for you. Pretty good deal, don't you think?

UltraKlear™ UVC

On the other hand if your pond is not naturally balanced, or lacks adequate filtration, then you'll likely experience symptoms like algae. This being the case, your next best choice is probably a UVC. However, presuming that you don't get overly intense (in that case you kill all kinds of things including the good and desirable aerobic bacteria) you can have a clarifying experience that will probably please the eye.

There are several drawbacks to the UV solution though. First, no matter how intense, UV clarifiers don't affect string algae at all, and so this problem is not addressed. Secondly, after the regular algae is killed, it generally falls to the bottom of the pond, biodegrades, and provides another wave of nutrition for another (often larger) algae bloom. If you're not careful, it's easy to encourage larger cycles of algae blooms by using a UVC. If your pond is unbalanced, the choices are minimal. The third, and most obvious drawback is that a UVC isn't cheap, and the bulbs usually require replacement every season.

4) Your pond must be at least three-feet deep in order to keep koi.

There are thousands of 2-foot-deep ponds around the country, full of happy and healthy koi. A common myth is that ponds must be built at least 3-feet deep, especially if they contain koi and/or are located in a colder climate. You see, the water in a 2-foot deep pond will only freeze eight inches down, even in the coldest of climates, because of the insulating qualities of the earth that surrounds the pond.

A pond that is too deep could be considered a swimming pool by your local government and therefore fall under strict guidelines and codes. Also, more digging means more work, more water to fill the pond, and more additives to treat algae and fish illnesses.

5) Koi can't be kept in a pond that also contains plants.

In a naturally balanced ecosystem, koi and plants complement and need one another. In nature, fish feed on plants. As a result, the fish produce waste, which is broken down by aerobic bacteria on the bottom of your pond, which, in turn, is used as fertilizer by the plants to grow and produce more natural fish food. It's known as the circle of life, and to imply that koi and plants shouldn't co-exist is to ignore nature.

On the contrary, fish naturally love to eat plants, and most of the time they'll (the fish) survive nicely without you feeding them at all … due to the plants and algae. On the other hand, you have to have a sufficient volume of plants to accommodate the koi too. In the naturally balanced pond, proportionality is always a key ingredient to success.

6) You have to bring your fish inside for the winter.

Fish do fine during the coldest of winters as long as you give them two feet of water to swim in, oxygenate the water, and keep a hole in the ice with a bubbler, allowing the naturally produced gasses to escape from under the ice. Otherwise, you let Mother Nature do the rest. The fish will spend the entire winter hibernating at the bottom of the pond and then they will slowly wake up as the water warms in the spring.

7) Your pond water must be tested on a daily basis.

This myth comes from the aquarium industry and it has a lot to do with the fact that an aquarium is a much smaller body of water and the small size makes it more difficult to balance. Mother Nature never tests her water, and her ecosystem does just fine. A well conceived, naturally balanced water garden normally requires no testing either.

Pond Equalizer balances the pH of the pond

But what if you're in balance and still have an excessive algae bloom, or your fish are having problems, and you suspect a pH imbalance? What then? You could have limestone rock in your pond. Limestone lowers the pH, increasing algae growth.

If all else fails, you can buy products specifically designed to bring pH to normal. The problem people have with these products is that it's really easy to overdose your pond and throw it into an acidic stage, which creates just as many problems (maybe more) as a high pH. The moral of the story is to, if at all possible, just work with Mother Nature and avoid having to fiddle with pH altogether. That's hard to beat!

8) A pond in your backyard means you will have a lot of mosquitoes.

Mosquitoes will generally only lay their eggs in still, stagnant water, not in moving water. If the mosquitos happen to lay eggs in your pond and the mosquito larvae hatch, the fish in your pond will consider them a treat and will pick them off the water's surface with great enthusiasm. Your skimmer will sweep up whatever the fish miss. Another option is to use a natural mosquito larvae killer, often known as Mosquito Dunks and PreStrike™.

Your skimmer will sweep up the excess leaves and mosquito larvae that the fish miss.

9) You cannot have a pond in an area where there are a lot of trees.

In nature, ponds and trees go together like ham and eggs on a breakfast table. Yes, you will have more leaves in your pond in the fall but, by the same token, the shade provided by the tree(s) will help minimize the algae bloom in the summer. Furthermore, if you have a skimmer sucking the top quarter inch of water off the top of your pond, it will pull most of the leaves and related debris into an awaiting net. This takes about 30 seconds to empty … and it can be a daily task in the fall if your pond is close to trees. Add it all up and it's a trade-off that most full-sun water gardeners would love to have! So don't worry about trees and ponds. They're fine.

10) You can't have koi in a pond that also has rocks and gravel.

Koi are actually just a fancy variety of carp and all carp, are bottom feeders. They love to swim along the bottom and scavenge everything that is available on and in between the rocks. In nature, it's not uncommon to find ponds, lakes, or rivers with rocks on the bottom. It's more like their natural environment than an exposed rubber liner, so why even think about doing battle with Mother Nature?

11) It's okay to use chemicals in your pond.

This one comes from the swimming pool industry. If chlorine is good for humans in the local swimming pool, then chemicals must be okay for fish and the plants in the pond. Products like algaecide (copper sulfate), dechlorinator (sodium thiosulfate), and fish antibiotics are commonly used as quick-fix solutions to balance related problems. In the end, your best bet is to attack the root cause of the problem and make sure that you have a naturally balanced pond that allows Mother Nature to take care of all the maintenance issues that she has so much experience with.

12) It's necessary to drain and clean your pond regularly.

The reality is, if you fail to set your system up so that it's working in harmony with Mother Nature, then you'll be asking for a lot of related problems which may require you to drain and clean your pond out on a regular basis. On the other hand, if you decide to work in harmony with Mother Nature instead of doing battle with her, then draining and cleaning your pond should take place only once a year (at most). Furthermore, it should happen in the spring before the weather gets warm and the bacteria has an opportunity to set up.

13) Bottom drains work best if you have koi.

The claim by many koi keepers is that the water will lack sufficient oxygen at the lower levels, and this insufficiency can be detrimental to your koi. The real fact is that if you avoid making your pond any deeper than two feet, there is very little difference in the oxygen levels at the surface and at the bottom of the pond. The problem with bottom drains is that they have a tendency to promote leaks, possibly leaving your fish landlocked. Now that's a problem to avoid at all costs.

Illustration by Michael P. Stout

14) The more filtration, the better the pond.

Believe or not, you can over-filter a pond. That's right. You can have such a tight filter pad in your skimmer that it picks up the smallest particles of debris, which will cause you to be cleaning the filtering mechanism out constantly. Now remember, we're not talking about drinking water here. What we are talking about is water clarity and water that's healthy for your fish. Fish in the wild certainly don't swim around in bottled water. If you can see a dime on the bottom of the pond, then the water clarity is just right for your fish and filtering past that is overkill and will create headaches, not eliminate them.

15) You can't be a koi hobbyist and a water gardener.

Not true! You can raise koi and have a beautiful water garden. There are koi hobbyists who have perfectly balanced pond ecosystems with no chemicals, no sterilization, and a nice assortment of plants. The koi can grow up to be just as beautiful and just as healthy as they are in traditional koi ponds — and you'll love them just as much!

16) High tech is the solution to controlling Mother Nature.

More than anything else, being observant and learning from Mother Nature is what it takes to be a water gardener. Whatever she does naturally is what you should be doing in your pond. Whatever she doesn't do is what you should be

avoiding in your pond. If there is a golden rule of pondering it is, not to mess with Mother Nature because you'll lose.

17) Small water features are less work.

As water features get larger, they actually become easier to maintain. Aquarium hobbyists know it's much easier to achieve a healthy, stable tank with more water, not less. Small water features rarely have the flow or capacity necessary for long-term stability, and soon need lots of maintenance. And so with ponds, bigger is always better.

18) You should never have algae in your pond.

Green algae, in proper proportion, is beneficial pond life. Fish eat it and it's part of the ecology of any living, healthy pond. Too much algae has two simple causes: too much accessible nutrition and too much sunlight. That's why a well-designed pond includes plenty of aquatic plants to compete for the available nutrition and shade from trees and aquatic plants.

19) Maintaining a water garden is a constant headache.

Ecologically-balanced water gardens let Mother Nature do the heavy lifting. Make sure the water garden you install works with Mother Nature, not against her. Including mechanical and biological filtration, lots of aquatic plants, fish, active bacteria, and plenty of rocks turn a high-maintenance headache into an enjoyable water garden experience.

20) A water garden costs a fortune.

A water garden is certainly an investment, but it no longer has to be a bottomless money pit. At the most affordable end of the spectrum, DIY kits with everything you need retail for under $1000, plus another $600 for the stuff that doesn't come in the box (rocks, pebbles, fish, and plants). Inexpensive fish and plants are easily found. Running a high efficiency pump 24 /7, 365 days a year, will tack about $25 to $40 onto your monthly electric bill. At the mid-range, you could expect to pay about the same for a average sized pond that you would pay to add a hot tub to your deck.

Chapter 4

Getting Started

What You Should Know Before Jumping In

You may have decided to put a beautiful water feature in your backyard, but feel a little overwhelmed with all the different philosophies, products, and literature on the subject. This is completely understandable, but getting started on building a pond should be an enjoyable experience — and it can be if you ask the right questions and get organized. The purpose of this chapter is to help you do just that. You must find a design, consider your budget, choose a site, and decide who should build your pond in order to get started with water gardening.

Do you want a lily pond, a mountain stream, or lakeside living?

Choosing the Pond Design

One of the most important aspects to consider when starting a project is the design. A good design brings both aesthetic value and functionality to the pond. Since there are so many ways of going about the design, it helps if you break them down into smaller, more manageable parts.

The first thing to consider is the original inspiration for the pond. Many times people see a stream or pond in nature that sparks their interest and they want their personal water feature to reflect this. For example, you may be looking for a rushing mountain stream like the ones you see in Colorado, or perhaps you are more of a lake person and want a large pond in which you can swim. Using any ideas you get from nature will help to create a truly unique and authentic-looking water feature. When designing your water feature, don't forget what inspired your decision to build a water garden.

Sizing up Your Pond

The next step is to decide on the size of the water garden you wish to install. There are a few limiting factors to consider when deciding how big your water feature should be. First off, it should be in scale with your house, the surrounding yard, landscaping, and hardscaping. In other words, don't create a water feature that encompasses the entire yard, leaving no room for sitting areas and surrounding landscape. It is important that the pond blend into the yard, not take it over.

Budget can also be a limiting factor. Remember that the materials needed to build the water feature make up only a portion of the total cost. Rock and labor (if you choose to hire someone) need to be added into the equation as well. Make sure you keep your finances in mind throughout the entire

A natural pond design

A formal pond design

design process. If you stay organized and keep track of costs as they add up, you should have no problem staying within your allotted budget.

Beyond the size constraints and budget factors, the size of the pond is pretty much up to you. Ponds can be made large enough to swim in, or small enough to fit in the tiniest city garden. They can never be too large!

Get in Shape

The shape of the pond is another aspect you will want to consider when planning your water feature. The shape is important because it helps to create the overall feel of the water feature. You may choose irregular, flowing lines (such as a kidney shape) that result in a more natural feature, or maybe you delight in geometric lines to create a more formal feel. Either way is fine, but just keep in mind how much of a difference the shape makes to the overall effect of the pond.

The Role of Plants

Plants play a very important role in the overall health of a water feature. Not only do they have an undeniable aesthetic value, but they also act as natural filters that help keep algae blooms under control. So it is no surprise that part of designing your water feature includes creating plenty of places to put aquatic plants.

One very simple way to achieve this is through proper excavation techniques. Since many aquatic plants thrive at different depths, creating several levels (or shelves) in the pond allows for the use of a variety of plants. One such example would be a group of aquatic plants called marginals, which prefer to be rooted in shallower waters.

A shelf that sits only 6 to 8" below the water surface would provide an ideal planting location for marginals. These shelves are covered with one to two inches of gravel, providing an ideal place to bury the root structures of your plants. During the excavation of the pond, small, crater-shaped depressions can be dug into the lowest shelf to accommodate for deeper water plants such as water lilies. Since the root structures of lilies tend to be rather large, the depressions help by providing areas of deeper gravel or soil, which will better support the plant. If a water feature does not have shelves or gravel, plants may still be used, however, they will need to remain in their original pots and your selection of plants may be more limited. In addition, without their root structures directly in the water, the plants will not be as effective at filtering the water. Bottom line, don't forget about the plants when designing your water feature.

Increased Circulation to Accomodate Dead Areas

In addition to creating a feel, the shape needs to be very functional as well. Since you will more than likely be circulating the water in the pond in order to keep it clean and healthy, you will want to avoid creating "dead areas."

These are areas created by sharp curves, which segregate certain parts of the pond from the main flow or current. In order to avoid this problem, try to keep a more open shape, free of drastic inlets and curves. Last, but not least, don't forget to consider your hardscapes when deciding on a shape. For example, you may want to curve the stream around a deck or patio for a more dramatic effect.

Again, turning to Mother Nature can help you with this decision if you desire a more natural feature. Look to the naturally occurring water features in your area for inspiration. Keeping these few guidelines in mind will help you choose a shape that is both beautiful and functional.

Dead Areas Eliminated by Alternate Shape

The Way the Water Flows

Streams and waterfalls are other considerations when designing your pond. Most people would agree that adding a stream or waterfall greatly increases the beauty and interest of the pond, but they also play a large role in the filtration of the pond. As water moves in a thin layer down the stream, it passes over a bed of gravel and through aquatic plants that pull out particles and debris. This process helps to cleanse the water. In addition, oxygen, which is necessary for many of the living organisms in the pond, such as the fish and bacteria, is gained as the water crashes down the stream and over the waterfall.

When adding a stream and waterfall to your pond, there are a few things you need to remember. First, you should have at least one inch of grade change for every 10 feet of stream in order to create the effect of moving water. If at all possible, you should also try to utilize the natural slope of the land. Second, make sure that your stream traverses back and forth across the landscape as much as possible. This not only creates a more interesting and natural look, but also increases the overall viewing area of the stream. Finally, your streams and waterfalls should always face or move toward the main viewing area. If you follow most, or all, of these basic tips you'll be able to create a natural-looking stream or waterfall to accentuate your water feature.

When adding a stream and waterfall to your pond, you should try to utilize the natural slope of the land.

Choosing the Site

Now that you have an idea of what you want your pond to look like and what it will include, it is time to make another important decision – where to put your water feature. How do you choose the best site for your pond? Like the design, there are a few standard guidelines that help simplify the process. Common sense can guide you in the right direction for this decision, however, there are also some common traps that people can get themselves into. Let's go over some of the major aspects that need to be considered.

Following a few major rules will help you choose the site for your pond. First, make sure the pond is visible from both the yard's outside seating areas, as well as your favorite rooms inside the house. Think about where you will spend most of your time. Even though you would like to go outside and enjoy your yard more, it is very likely that much of your time at home is spent in the living room or kitchen. In this case, wouldn't it be nice if you could glance out your window and see your fish swimming around? Wouldn't it be relaxing to sit in your favorite chair or at the dinner table and view a beautiful waterfall crashing down over the rocks?

Keep It Close

When you are outside, you should not have to walk far out into your yard or leave the areas where you and your friends are most likely to congregate to enjoy your water feature. This brings us to the second most important rule,

Your stream and waterfall should always face or move toward the main viewing area.

which is to bring the feature up close to the hardscape. If you decide to go out and enjoy a relaxing summer evening, or have some friends over (for a barbecue) it is unlikely that you (or your company)

will wander very far from the deck or patio. So having your water feature up close where you and your friends can feed the fish and hear the waterfall is very important.

Other Considerations

Oftentimes, people will see a low area of their yard where water already tends to collect and think that area would be a great place for a pond – after all, it already holds water, right? Actually, this area would be a bad spot for a water garden. Ground water can build up underneath the liner and cause it to bubble up above the surface of the water and shift. The area is also likely to receive runoff from rainwater that often contains lawn chemicals, which can either hurt your fish or cause excessive algae bloom. It's best to keep your water garden on higher ground if at all possible.

Choosing a location that has a natural slope to work with is something else to consider. This is not the most important criteria, but if there is a natural slope that moves toward the viewing area, it should be utilized. The slope can greatly aid in creating a natural-looking stream or waterfall.

All of this information may seem a little overwhelming, but as long as you do some research of your own and plan ahead for your water feature, everything should fall into place.

Planning Ahead for Your Water Feature

There are a few things that you can do to get ready before you install your water feature. It is always a good idea to look through as many pictures of naturally

It's best to keep your water garden on higher ground if at all possible.

occurring water features as possible to get ideas for your own water garden. Then, you can make a more informed and confident decision about what you want in your own backyard. Talk to people who already have water features in their backyards and generate a list of pros and cons. The last thing you want to do is jump in headfirst and rush the pond design.

As long as you are thinking ahead, try to incorporate any future landscape or hardscape plans into your design. Do your homework, and your resulting pond will be well thought out and organized.

Are You a Do-It-Yourselfer?

Now that you have an idea of the design and location of the water garden you want, there is still one final question. Do you want to tackle this project yourself or let a hired professional take control? In order to answer this question, you have to understand just how much

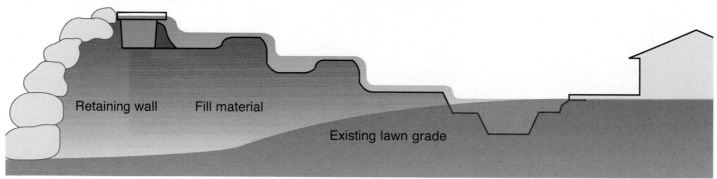

Your stream and water garden should always face or move toward the viewing area. Also, it's best to keep your water garden on higher ground, if possible.

Chapter 4 - Getting Started

work is involved in building a pond, and whether or not you're ready to tackle such a project.

The bottom line is, in order to install your own water feature, you should be prepared for a great deal of physical labor. Building a pond usually involves digging a decent-sized hole and placing a few tons of rock and gravel. So, needless to say, it's not easy work. However, you may be the kind of person who enjoys a challenge – a "weekend warrior."

The kind of person that would build their own pond would exhibit a few key character traits. They would need to be

have to enjoy a good physical challenge. If you happen to fit the above description, then building your own water feature would be an exciting challege for you.

On the other hand, you may be the kind of person who would rather leave this kind of thing to the professionals. People who choose to hire out the labor share some common characteristics as well. They may not be in the best physical shape, and might not have picked up a shovel in a good many years. They may not have any landscape or pond building experience, both of which come in handy for a project like this. Also, they may not

The Rocks Make a Difference

Rocks, like the plants, have a dual role in both the aesthetics and function of a water feature. Different types of rock can greatly affect the design of your pond. With so many types to choose from, and taking into consideration the dramatic difference in indigenous rock across the country, it is impossible to name one type as the best for a water feature. However, there are some general guidelines to help you choose the right rock for the situation. First, try to use rock that occurs naturally in the area – this helps to tie the feature in with the surrounding landscape. Next, try not to mix different types of rock or it can make the pond look thrown together and unattractive. Finally, and most importantly, make sure to get varying sizes of whatever rock you are going to use in the feature. The best ratio is 1:2:1 (1 part small, 2 parts medium, and 1 part large). The varying sizes of rocks help to give each other scale – the large stones only look large because there are small stones surrounding it, and vice versa.

in pretty good physical shape and love to design and build things with their own two hands. This person would not be afraid of taking their time and making the occasional mistake. They would also need to have the time to devote to seeing the project through, which may take up a few consecutive weekends. Finally, and perhaps most importantly, they would

be very handy building things or with hands-on projects in general. Time is also a consideration; some people want or need the project done in a reasonable amount of time, and done right the first time. Finally, a person may just want the experience of a seasoned pond builder and they don't really care if they have a hand in it.

In addition, using different size stones adds visual interest to the feature and helps differentiate it from man-made structures like retaining walls. The stone's function in a water feature is to add support, possibly protect any liner from harmful UV rays, and give beneficial microorganisms a place to grow. Taking these guidelines into consideration, it is up to you to choose the color, shape, and texture of stone that most suits you and the look that you want to achieve.

A professional installer can also save you a lot of money in bad decisions.

Show Me the Money!

Cost can also be an important factor when deciding whether or not to build the pond yourself. So, which way really is cheaper? It may seem that by doing it yourself you would save a lot of money on labor and that's all there is to it. There are a couple of different ways to look at it, however, so make sure you understand what true costs are involved with both options.

By building the water feature yourself, you will save a lot of money on labor. Lets face it, labor is about a third of the cost of putting in a water feature. There are a few loopholes in this line of thinking, however, that need to be taken into consideration. First you have to decide what your time is worth. If weekends are your time to spend with your family, or your time to get things done around the house, building a pond may be difficult to fit in your schedule. Also, remember that any mistakes you make are on your dime. This means that any changes

that need to be made or extra materials that need to be purchased are going to cost you, not the contractor. If you use hired labor you may pay more initially, but may actually end up saving money in the long run. Any mistakes that are made would be the responsibility of the installer, and the installer would foot the bill for them.

Time to Get Started!

You now have all the information you need to get started on your new water feature. Take your time, plan ahead, and don't forget to utilize the tips and information given in this chapter. Make sure to place great importance on designing and locating your pond, because it can make or break the project. Don't forget the important extras like plants and streams. And, if you are planning on doing it yourself, you might want to start lifting weights as soon as possible. ✐

Chapter 5

Filtering Through Your Options

Choosing the Right Equipment for the Project

With so many different forms of filtration out there, your head must be spinning. From common kinds of filtration, referred to as mechanical and biological filters, to other forms of filtration, it's best to learn a few of the basic options so you can make an educated decision about your water garden filtration system.

The Skimmer Basics

Skimmers, also referred to as mechanical filters, are a huge part of your pond's ecosystem. Sure, they might not look as cool as your gushing waterfall or eat out of your hand like your favorite koi, but they do take care of a lot of the

> *The foundation for any good skimmer lies in its construction. Rotational molded polyethylene is the best choice in terms of structure because it is durable, yet flexible.*

debris in your pond. This debris could be harmful to your fish and make your waterfall look less than stellar.

Skimmers house and protect the pump, ridding your water garden of larger particles, waste, and sediment. There are many types of filters designed to perform this task, and that's why it can be so difficult to distinguish between the good and the bad.

There are two main types of skimmers — box and floating. Both types filter water by removing debris and waste before it has had a chance to fall to the bottom of the pond — much like a swimming pool filter. The box skimmer is the one you'll see the most of because it's the easiest to maintain.

You Need Structure
The foundation for any good skimmer lies in its construction. There are four common filter manufacturing techniques, including rotational molded poly, fiberglass, blow-molded plastic, and vacuum formed. Rotational molded polyethylene is the best choice in terms of structure because it is durable, yet flexible. Fiberglass is a little too rigid, and may be prone to cracking, especially in winter months. Blow-molded plastic has weak points in the corners of the filter, compromising its strength and structural stability. Vacuum forming minimizes thickness making it too flexible, causing performance problems. Also, since it is stretched out of a flat sheet of plastic, the corners can be very weak.

Size and Shape Matter
The shape and height of your skimmer is also very important. There are different styles of skimmers out there and you need to remember that some may not leave you with very many pump options. For example, when the skimmer is in the shape of a bell, there is ample space near the bottom of the skimmer, but the fact that it narrows at the top may limit your pump choices. As for the height of a skimmer, if it is too short, you may have big problems with your pump. If the pump sits too close to the water level and you have any sort of water flow restriction (clogged nets or mats), the pump can suck the reservoir dry and overheat. This will shorten the life of your pump.

"Weir" All in This Together
The next thing you'll want to look at is the weir, which is the flap found in the skimmer opening that controls the amount of water that goes in and out of the skimmer. First of all, you need to make sure that it is in a reasonable spot so that it can skim the top of the water. Misplacement of the weir may reduce the amount of water flowing into the skimmer, also reducing the overall ability of the filter to effectively skim the surface of the water. Another style skimmer has an accordion-like weir

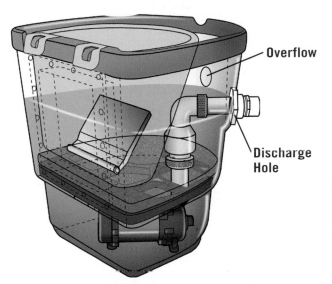

Make sure that the skimmer's overflow is below the pump discharge hole so the water only escapes through that opening.

that can be closed to drain the skimmer for easy (and dry) maintenance. This would be great if the closing mechanism didn't slip from the water pressure and open, filling the skimmer up quickly – meaning you'd better get your clean-out work done quickly! It provides excellent skimming, but the long-term durability is in question. Since it is made of a stitched flexible membrane and not a strong material like plastic, its lifespan is shorter.

Overflowing With Options

Another thing that would be helpful to look for when deciding on the skimmer is the overflow. Some models don't have an overflow hole in the back – that can be a real problem. The overflow is designed to keep your pond from flooding after heavy rains or any other watery disasters. The last thing you want is to walk out to your backyard and see your fish flopping around on the lawn. Some models have an overflow that is too close to the discharge, which may direct water to the wrong hole, causing your skimmer to float. You'll want to make sure that the overflow is below the pump discharge hole so the water only escapes through that opening. A little bit of research could mean the difference between worry and relaxation.

Debris Nets and Baskets

When it comes to debris nets and baskets, both can be very good for your skimmer. A mesh net with an aluminum support is very easy to remove from the skimmer, flip over, and dump out debris. The aluminum support is important to keep the net in place so it collects debris correctly and doesn't get tangled. There is also the option of a plastic basket, which is also very useful. However, with the basket, the sturdiness of some skimmers could come into play. If your skimmer bows inward, it could be very difficult to remove the basket, so pay close attention to the structure that will be housing it.

Filtering Without Clogs

One of the biggest debates in the water gardening industry has to do with horizontal vs. vertical filter mats. Horizontal mats came first, and were soon followed by the vertical filter mat, providing the customer with a pull-out tray for easier access. Once again, the sturdiness of the mold is in question; the last thing you want to be doing is tugging to get that tray out after ground pressure has wedged it firmly into place. Putting the tray back into the skimmer could be a whole separate nightmare. You also have to make sure the vertical filter mat is clean at all times. If the filter is clogged, the water will not flow through and the water level will be lowered, which could mean trouble for your pump.

The horizontal mat, on the other hand, allows water to flow through freely and lays flat on the support rack, meaning less wear and tear.

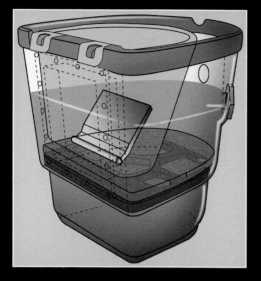

Horizontal Filter Mat

The horizontal mat design was created in the field as the first professional pond skimmer. It's breezed through the test of time, showing why it's still the #1 selling skimmer on the market today. Now entering its 7th generation, the horizontal design is still standing at the top of the mountain, and here's why.

Design Benefits of the Horizontal Filter Mat:
- Allows water to pass evenly through the mat.
- Made of sturdy materials and evenly balanced on the support rack.
- Traps all smaller debris that passes through the net.
- Lays flat so there is no sagging or early wear and tear.
- Never clogs to the point of preventing water from passing through, so the pump chamber does not run dry.
- An automatic water fill valve can be used without the worry of excess water being introduced into the system.

Maintenance of the Horizontal Filter Mat:
- Cleaning once a month, if needed.
- May have to replace the mat every three years.

Put a Lid On It
It's hard to believe that the lid of the skimmer could be such a big deal, but aesthetically, some of the designs can be scary. After working so hard to make your new pond blend into your backyard, you aren't going to want an unnatural lid made of black plastic covering your skimmer.

A lid that resembles a natural stone is your best bet. You'll also want to make sure that it is capable of withstanding some pressure, yet lightweight for ease of use. Whether you want them to or not, people might stand on the lid to get a better view of your pond, and if it can't withstand their weight, you've got a big problem.

Keep It Simple
The bottom line when it comes to choosing your skimmer is to keep things simple. A basic design is always the best way to go. When things start getting complicated, with two separate chambers or several different kinds of filtration, there are more opportunities for failure.

Simplicity will make a big difference when you're enjoying your low-maintenance, chemical-free water garden in the privacy of your own backyard. You'll be glad you did the research now, so you don't have to deal with the problems later.

What Is a Biological Filter?
A good biological filtration system, teamed up with a mechanical filter that removes solids before the water enters the biological filtration system, is the most effective way to filter water. As the water enters the biological filter, it flows up through filtration media such as filter mats and lava rock. The final step is

to make sure that there is enough oxygen going back into the pond - that's where the waterfall or stream comes into play.

Now that's enough of all that technical mumbo-jumbo ... in simple terms, biological filtration helps Mother Nature by providing a large amount of surface area for the bacteria to latch on to and multiply. As the water is drawn through the filter, the bacteria helps remove the excess nutrients.

The Way Mother Nature Intended

Now, it is important to realize that no one can play Mother Nature, but a balanced ecosystem can imitate the basic philosophies and actions of that wise woman. Your filter is the key to that balance.

Your best bet is to search for a filter with a square frame made of rotational-molded polyethylene, the perfect base for building a beautiful, convincing, leak-free waterfall, with all of the right components. You'll also want to look for a complete package — including filter mats, a media net, a filter support rack, a bulkhead, and a waterfall stone — everything you need for a truly spectacular waterfall.

The built-in rock ledge of some filters allow them to be completely camouflaged and out of sight. The rock ledge must be wide enough to support rocks, making it fairly simple to foam them into place, hiding the filter for a natural-looking waterfall.

Some filters either don't have a ledge, have a ledge that's too narrow, or they provide a shelf that must be purchased separately. While plants in the filter can cover a majority of the rim, what happens in the spring when the foliage is not thick enough or in the fall when those plants thin out? A rock ledge is a must when creating an aesthetically pleasing waterfall, using a biological filter.

photo by Robert Osler

That's the Way the Water Flows

Whether you want a waterfall reminiscent of your trip to Niagara Falls, or a trickling drip that reminds you of a small mountain spring, in water gardening, water flow is everything! Both the pump and the size of your biological filter determine the flow rate of the water. Another important feature is the size of the spillway, which is the opening where the water flows into the pond.

Some filters have spillways that are way too small to handle the amount of water they promise. In fact, some have spillways that are less than 12 inches wide. This limits the waterfall flow to 1000 gallons per hour, which could cause water to spill over the sides, resulting in excessive water loss.

Stone Cold

When it comes to the beauty of your waterfall, what is one of the most important things that can make or break the design? The waterfall stone is one key! While it seems fairly simple, waterfall stones can have problems. They are often sold separately and can be extremely heavy, or hard to work with. Some stones are so heavy that, although other rocks were placed around it, the lip still leaned forward.

When the biological filters come with the stone screwed directly into the unit, you don't have the choice to use a natural stone in its place. A lightweight, optional waterfall stone is very realistic looking, but also gives people the opportunity to use a real rock in the design.

There's no Substitute for Experience

Make sure you purchase your pond supplies from a reputable company that knows what they're doing, provides you with good products, and has the experience and knowledge to back their claims. Don't choose one that is perfectly willing to sell you anything, just for the sake of profit. Question them about the product you are about to buy and make sure that it will truly benefit your aquatic paradise. Prove that you know more than they think you do. Ask them about the environment of ponds, and stress that you want a naturally balanced ecosystem.

Many companies offer inexpensive water garden products that may look good, but fail one simple test ... the test of time. For strong, quality products that won't fail you throughout the years, shop for a quality system. Although it can be pretty tempting to go for the price break, you and your pond can end up suffering drastically. You get what you pay for!

Other Forms of Filtration

It's important to note that not every filter falls into either the mechanical or biological filter categories. Many of them have dual uses, and can be considered both biological and mechanical. In fact, box filters like the ones already mentioned, are also considered "bio-mechanical."

Pre-Filter

A pre-filter is a filter box that attaches directly to the pump in the water. It then filters the water directly as

A rock ledge made it possible to disguise this biological filter while bags of lava rock or BioBalls™ increase filter capacity and can be easily removed for cleaning on an annual basis..

UV clarifiers can provide the "quick fix" some people are looking for.

it comes into the pump. After the water is filtered, it is shot out of a fountain or into tubing, to a stream or a waterfall. These are high maintenance filters that require frequent (sometimes daily or more) cleanouts. It generally sits in the middle of your pond, and if your water is clear, they are very unnatural and aesthetically unattractive. They are basically safe for your critters with the exception of tadpoles and very small fish that may get caught in the filter.

UV Light

An ultraviolet light is a form of filtration that uses light to help water clarity. UV lights are commonly categorized into two types — sterilizers and clarifiers. The clarifier has a low wattage bulb and is used to disrupt the growth and reproductive cycle of single cell algae and clear up pea-soup green water. A sterilizer has a higher wattage and may kill beneficial organisms in your pond. UV lights should be replaced, on average, once a year. Flow rate and exposure times are critical when it comes to UV lights. Much like a tanning bed, where increased exposure time will work better, water passing through them too quickly will not be cleaned as effectively.

In-Line Box Filter

An in-line box filter runs pond water through a single box, or a series of box filters, filled with a different variety of media, ranging from lava rock and foam filter pads, to brushes and plastic shavings. These kinds of filters are generally large and cumbersome. They can be buried underground, (and covered with man hole type covers) or housed above ground and hidden behind a berm, or in a building to minimize the unnatural looking results. In-line box filters can be prone to clogging, reduced water flow, and other maintenance problems if regular cleaning is postponed.

Canister filter

Canister Filter

Canister filters force water into a sealed container, which is filled with various forms of media (plastic shavings, bioballs or foam filter pads). Due

Bubble bead filter

to the density of the media, canister filters have a tendency to clog up frequently when solid debris from a pond is forced through them. And when clogging occurs, water flow is drastically reduced. This forces the owner to clean the filter in order to keep the pond running. Typically, cleaning a filter of this sort, requires dismantling the filter and washing off the media. This makes them difficult and time-consuming to clean.

Bubble Bead Filter

A bubble bead filter features an external biofilter consisting of a molded PVC canister that contains some type of media, generally plastic beads. The water flows up through the filter and is cleaned biologically, and then it's flushed back into the pond. A UV clarifier is sometimes used with this system. The filter chamber has to be back-flushed regularly (minimally once a week) in order for

it to function properly. They are large (some get up to 10 feet tall), unnatural looking, sit outside your pond, and are very difficult (almost impossible) to camouflage. They're relatively safe for pond critters, and they're generally on the expensive side.

Sand Filter

A sand filter is a mechanical filtration system that was invented for swimming pools, not ponds. In a swimming pool where you have little to no solid debris, a sand filter works well. Ponds, however, are slightly different. There's fish waste, organic debris from decomposing aquatic plant material, and many more suspended solids in pond water. Sand filters act like very fine nets or filter cloths that allow liquid, but prohibit solids from passing through. Sand filters in the typical backyard pond will clog rapidly. These are super high maintenance and require frequent (occasionally several times per day) backwashing. It also sits outside your pond, is unnatural looking, and very difficult to hide. The frequent backwashing can undermine working bacteria, upsetting the ecosystem's balance, which can also be counterproductive to your critters. Furthermore, a sand filter is just plain expensive.

The Rest of the Story

Make sure you are careful not to overload your pond. A good filtration system will encompass both mechanical and biological filtering capabilities. It is synthesis that dictates clear water in your pond. Enjoy your aquatic paradise! 🖋

Chapter 6

The Pond-to-Fish Equilibrium

Fish in Your Water Garden

by Dr. Erik Johnson

Perhaps the most important "fundamental" of fish and pond care is your understanding that a balanced equilibrium, or ecosystem, must exist in the water feature. The ecosystem represents a successful balance among the fish and their needs, the pond's appearance, your needs, and the ability of the pond to support those fish. Simply, you must create and maintain a balanced ecosystem, or there will be problems among the fish, or in the pond.

Why Fish?

Fish are desired for the hobbyist's pond because they add color and interest to the water garden. With the exception of tempting your senses, plants are neither interactive nor friendly, while fish are both of these things, especially at feeding time. I've never seen plants crowding the surface, waving their leaves for your attention or fertilizer tablets. Of course, fish are also attractive, interesting, and even personable. Their color can enhance the visual impact of a pond. Koi in particular, as a species, grow very large, and their sheer size adds an impressive element to some water features (but not without a significant impact on the balanced ecosystem.)

Fish are friendly and interactive at feeding time.

What Fish?

There are numerous types of fish that you could put in your pond. You should make an informed decision about the type of fish you choose to make sure it's the right choice for you and your pond. There are various non-technical categories of fish: Scavengers, Supporting Cast, and Stars of the Show.

Scavengers

Snails, catfish, and the algae-eating plecostomus will figure into this category. Snails are enjoyable and harmless to fish. They control algae on the surfaces of the pond bottom, rocks, and plants. They are trouble-free and can become very numerous.

Ramshorn snails tend to be very sensitive to water temperature and quality, so they may end up making more of a mess through their death and decay than they might help. Trapdoor snails are really enjoyable, hardy to cold water, and interesting. Trapdoor snails reproduce VERY slowly, so they never become a nuisance.

Catfish are sometimes used in ponds as scavengers, but they end up eating fish food and helping very little with clean up. Catfish can also damage valuable koi and goldfish, especially if they get a hankering for fish eyes. Yes,

Trapdoor snail

channel catfish can sometimes sample a fish eye, and, enjoying it immensely, proceed to clean out the heads of every fish in the pond.

Plecostomus are tropical algae eaters that work very well in ornamental ponds, clearing algae from the pond bottom. They are territorial, so only one should be used in the average pond. In one instance, two large (12") specimens were used in a 6,000 gallon pond and that was two too many. The pair ate ALL of the carpet-algae, and the ecosystem was destabilized. Plecostomus are tropical fish, which means that while they will thrive in your pond during the summer, they will die in the fall. Their breaking point is exactly 55°F. At a water temperature of 56°F, they will be stiff and inverted, but salvageable if you quickly move them indoors. When the temperature drops one more degree, they summarily die.

Supporting Cast

Fish which function aesthetically as the "supporting cast" would be fish that add interest without being the "star of the show." Notable examples include the mosquito fish (*Gambusia affinis*) and the red belly dace. Both fish can carry disease, without appearing sick at all. These should not be used in a pond with valuable fish.

Plecostomus are tropical algae eaters that work very well in ornamental ponds, clearing algae from the pond bottom.

However, in water features where koi and goldfish are not important, mosquito fish are very enjoyable. They are highly reproductive and busy, always eating mosquito larvae and anything else that falls in the pond. They can overwinter and are durable to most pond shortcomings in terms of water quality. Red belly dace are attractive, active, and durable, however they are more sensitive to water quality issues than the mosquito fish.

Stars of the Show

The "stars of the show" are goldfish and koi!

Koi: These are large carp which have been bred by the Japanese for hundreds of years. Over the last several decades, the selection of the color patterns and varieties have tripled. There's hardly a color you can imagine that you couldn't find

Fish add beauty and interest to water features.

in koi. Koi grow up to 40 inches in length (larger exceptions exist), and some enjoy uprooting potted plants.

To choose a valuable koi, the beginner is advised to purchase fish with bold color patterns. If you spy a red and white fish you like, look for bold white and a bold red without blurring of the colors. Avoid fish with freckles of the principal color throughout the white. Finally, the pattern, while bold, should be balanced from left to right and from front to back.

photo by Robert Osler

The Sarassa features a white base color and brilliant red highlights. The Sarassa may have come from a cross between the Red Cap Oranda and the comet goldfish.

The same is true for black and white fish. Bold patterning, no blurring, no freckles, and good balance are key characteristics to look for. Beyond these guidelines in the evaluation of most fish, there are other elements of body shape, patterning and the distribution of color.

Goldfish: These occur in numerous, different types from the lowly "comet" goldfish (orange plain) to the Japanese oranda, the Japanese ranchu, the Chinese lionhead, the ryukin and so on. It would not be inaccurate to assert that almost any inexpensive goldfish will do well in your outdoor pond, while a more costly, or highly refined Japanese goldfish, such as the ryukin or oranda will probably suffer from illness if left outside over winter. This is even truer with the adults of these exotic varieties. The reason for this "over-winter-weakness" is related to the compacted, distended abdomen of the expensive, select varieties. Their abdomens are a delicate balancing act of a downward ballast, the intestine, and plenty of fat. The hardship of winter almost always degrades this equilibrium, causing adult orandas to flip over and eventually perish.

Shubunkin

Fish add beauty and interest to water features.

you DEFINITELY need a filter, but if you only feed them once or twice per week, the fish will grow slowly and will probably not (as far as waste goes) exceed the environmental carrying capacity of the pond.

Selecting Healthy Fish

Notice the water the fish are in — it almost doesn't matter how healthy the fish may look at the store, if the water stinks or appears cloudy or hazy, those fish are GOING to be sick, or harbor serious disease. Cloudy water is usually a symptom of bacterial overgrowth and this is a serious stress to the fish. These bacterial blooms usually lead to secondary-infections in the fish exposed. Poor water conditions easily and quickly cause disease.

Notice the appetite of the fish. Fish should eat aggressively in the facilities at the retail center. Healthy koi found in nice, warm water will be in constant motion, looking for food. When food is placed on the surface of the tank, the fish should swarm for it. If the fish are

Any fish with a mark or sore represents the overall health of the other fish.

Basic Ground Rules

If you have never owned a water garden before and you know nothing about maintaining fish, then remember the following basic ground rules:

First, the fish need good, clean water. If you have children, there is a simple way to evaluate (at a glance) the suitability of the pond. If you wouldn't let them wade in the pond, then it's not good enough for fish, either. The water should be clean-smelling. Clarity of the water right down to the bottom is good and a yellowing of the deeper water is bad. Green water is okay, but it can be troublesome. Water can be kept "clean" enough with a filter. Even if there is no filter, there MUST be some water movement, like from a water pump, which does little more than add circulation to improve oxygen exchange. This is CRUCIALLY important in the summertime when water temperatures are over 60°F.

Second, fish that are maintained in outdoor ponds can obtain nutrition from a variety of natural sources, such as wayward insects and plants, but they need a prepared (staple) food at least once per week. If you choose to feed the fish every day, motionless on the tank bottom or they ignore the feeding time, consider other fish, or visit the fish the next day before

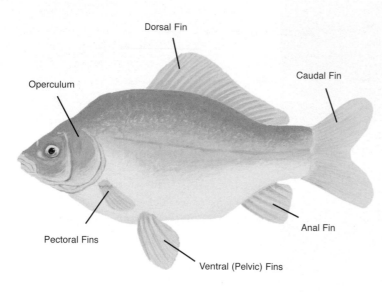

Dorsal Fin

Caudal Fin

Operculum

Anal Fin

Pectoral Fins

Ventral (Pelvic) Fins

purchasing one of them. Perhaps they will be better or worse, which would simplify your assessment.

Look for marks on the fish. Any fish with a mark or sore represents the overall health of the other fish. All fish should be unblemished. If one fish has a broken fin from shipment, you should realize that all the fish were equally mishandled. If a fish has a bacterial infection or sore on it, then you should recognize that all the fish were exposed to the conditions which caused the bacterial infection to occur in the first place. Poor water conditions and/or parasites could be the cause of damage to the skin.

Finally, look at how the fish swim. Dorsal and caudal fins should generally be erect. It's one of the oldest adages in the fish business, but it's also very true. When a fish feels poorly, it will spend a considerable amount of time with its fins clamped to its sides. Do not buy fish in this condition, and do not buy fish that are maintained in the same water as these fish! Even if the fish only have a simple parasitism, you don't want to buy a problem.

Buying on the Internet

In general, I would discourage buying fish on the Internet because it's a leap of faith to get the particular fish you want combined with the good health you're looking for. For many people, however, there aren't any other options. For quite a few people, their hometown does not have any sort of dealer of pond fish. In even more localities, there isn't a quality dealer of very good and beautiful high-end koi. In these cases, the Internet can afford better prices and selection than you might find locally. There are as many good dealers on the Internet as there are bad dealers. On some of the online auction sites, I have seen koi being sold for two and three times what their quality and health dictate they should cost. People are being ripped off in some cases. It is difficult to assess the actual quality and health of a fish being sold online, so very reputable sources should be chosen and relied upon. Warranties and satisfaction policies become important, so look for them. Reputable dealers should be able to furnish references and cite a long history of selling healthy fish. Word of mouth may be your best guide.

Feeding

If you want your fish to grow fast, and large, then you would want to feed them more, and do more water changes. This is true even if you possess a very good filtration system. Feeding several times per day produces more waste and is hard for the

natural ecosystem to balance against. The equilibrium comes from a combination of filtration, water changes, and plant nitrate reduction. For best results, and maximum growth, use a food, that principally contains fishmeal as the top ingredient. Feed the fish two to three times per day. During a feeding, allow all the food the fish want to eat in about four to five minutes, and stop feeding when ANY food remains floating on the surface after these few minutes have passed.

If you do NOT want the fish to grow fast, then you would feed less and not push. their growth. Even in cases where the pond is heavily planted, feeding once or twice per week may not be sufficient unless there is an abundance of insects and other material entering the pond. Watch for signs of thinness in the fish, and weakness or disappearance in the smaller fish. If seen, you should be feeding more. The die-hard belief that fish have to be fed daily is absolutely not true. In my planted water garden, I feed the koi and goldfish twice per week.

Krill provide an excellent treat in addition to a staple food.

The concept of big water and crowding densities is also important. It's not something you do as a form of management, but an action item you should be alert to. Paying attention to overcrowding will make you a smashing success because it's a commonly abused variable with fish. You should have no more than one inch of fish per 10 gallons of pond water.

It's really that simple. If you have more fish than that, you have created a more difficult (and risky) equilibrium to maintain. It can be done, but you will find it a struggle with many possible failures. If you have less than one inch of fish per 10 gallons of water, then you would have better luck and better growth among your fish.

In a disease outbreak, the venerable Dr. John Gratzek offers this simple, but sage, advice: "Spread 'em out." He's right! By doing so, you are giving the fish more of what they want – space – and hampering the pathogens in their spread from fish to fish.

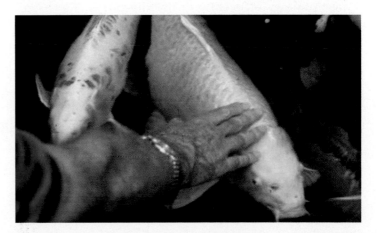

Other Environmental Problems:

Overheating

Overheating is common in ponds that are either in full sun, or located in the southwest United States. Ponds warmer than 80°F should be considered "overheated," and with this perfectly-acceptable condition come the following very-real risks.

In an overheated pond, oxygen depletion is not only possible, but likely. To avoid this, the pond should be well aerated or circulated. Fish ponds will not last long without aeration or water circulation when overheated.

Even if the pond is well aerated, an overheated pond contains overheated fish. It's important not to stress the fish when they're overheated. This is particularly true of large female fish. Kept scarcely warmer than 80°F and then presented with a stressor, they can dash 20 yards and summarily die.

Supercooling

Supercooling is a common spring and fall phenomena you should avoid. Your waterfall, coupled with a wide day-night temperature cycle, is the culprit here. Super cooling cases are common in Reno, Nevada, and North Carolina where the daytime temperatures might achieve 80°F and then freeze again at night. (Desert or mountain range phenomena). The waterfall and pond will pick up heat (radiant and ambient) during the day and then, still running at night, will discharge this heat. This is because water gives and takes energy efficiently in its thin-phase. For example, a cup of coffee stays warm in its cup, but poured back and forth from cup to cup, it cools rapidly. So your waterfall cools and heats the water. Any 20°F drop or rise in temperature in a single day is stressful to the fish, and, sooner-than-later, can result in sick, vulnerable fish. The trick in the spring or fall is to run the waterfall by day and capitalize on the free solar heating. Then, perhaps via a light-sensor or even a thermostat, arrange the waterfall to stop at nightfall when it gets cold, conserving heat in the pond where it belongs.

Heron attacks are oftentimes traumatic, if not fatal.

Trauma

Trauma is not a disease entity per se, however, from time to time these problems do occur. Trauma is usually associated with the spawning ritual in the springtime. The fish interact with each other pretty roughly, and abrasions from rocks and other pond ornamentation are common. If the pond water is warmer than 60°F, and the water quality tests well, then you should see these healing spontaneously. Other forms of trauma, like heron attacks and leaps from the pond to the ground, should be handled on a case-by-case basis, but usually revolve around the customary care for bacterial infections.

Pathogens

Pathogens of fish include parasites, bacteria, fungal infections, and even viral infections. Parasites should be considered as simply as possible. In your backyard, understand that there are different types of parasites, but they're treated as (and within) broad classes, with the safest possible remedies.

Diseases

There are some common diseases that can be identified and treated. The following chart will go a long way when you are confused and unsure what to do for your ailing fish.

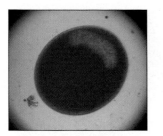
Ick

Chilodonella

Flukes

Pathogen	Simplest remedy	Advanced remedy	If plants are involved	If goldfish would be impacted
Ick	Salt 0.3% for five to seven days. In cold water, this could require seven days or more. In warm water, this will only require three days. EcoRx™ and Ick Control are also good remedies.	High heat or removal of all fish can work. Ick requires a host within a few days, and cannot tolerate temperatures over (85ºF).	Remove plants. Salt is the single best remedy for Ick because Ick exists under the skin for several days, requiring a long term remedy.	No.
Costia	Salt 0.6% for five to seven days.	Potassium permanganate can work in cases where salt is not acceptable or effective. Formalin is also very effective.	Remove plants. Remove all fish to a separate tank for two or three "once daily" 120 minute Formalin treatments. Leave system fishless for 14 days and double dose potassium permanganate several times to kill free forms.	No.
Trichodina	Salt 0.6% for five to seven days.	Potassium permanganate can work in cases where salt is not acceptable or effective. Formalin is also very effective.	Remove plants. Remove all fish to a separate tank for two or three "once daily" 120 minute Formalin treatments. Leave system fishless for 14 days and double dose potassium permanganate several times to kill free forms.	All referenced remedies at left are safe for goldfish.
Chilodonella	Salt 0.3% for five to seven days.	Potassium permanganate can work in cases where salt is not acceptable or effective. Formalin is also very effective.	Remove plants. Remove all fish to a separate tank for two or three "once daily" 120 minute Formalin treatments. Leave system fishless for 14 days and double dose potassium permanganate several times to kill free forms.	All referenced remedies at left are safe for goldfish.

Pathogen	Simplest remedy	Advanced remedy	If plants are involved	If goldfish would be impacted
Epistylis /Scyphidia	Salt 0.3% for five to seven days.	Potassium permanganate can work in cases where salt is not acceptable or effective. Formalin is also very effective.	Remove all fish to a separate tank for two or three "once daily" 120 minute Formalin treatments. Leave main system fishless for 14 days and double dose potassium permanganate in that main system several times to kill free forms.	All referenced remedies at left are safe for goldfish.
Flukes	EcoRx™ Parasite Control	Remove all fish to a separate tank for two or three "once daily" 120 minute Formalin treatments. Leave main system fishless for 14 days and double dose potassium permanganate in that main system several times to kill free forms.	SupaVerm and Prazi do not harm plants.	Praziquantel is safe for Goldfish while SupaVerm most definitely is NOT.
Bacterial Infections	EcoRx™ Anti-Bacteria	Injections of antibiotics, plus medicated food for all other fish.	All referenced remedies at left are safe for plants.	All referenced remedies at left are safe for goldfish.
Fungal Infections	EcoRx™ Fungus Control	Potassium permanganate.	Skip the salt part if you have sensitive plants. Usually, simple heat and good water quality are fundamentally enough for fungal control.	All referenced remedies at left are safe for goldfish.

Common pond health questions

1. I cannot get my pH down. What should I do?

Nothing. A high pH doesn't matter unless there are high ammonia levels to complicate the situation. Fish don't mind a pH as high as 9.0 or 10.0 as long as everything else is stable.

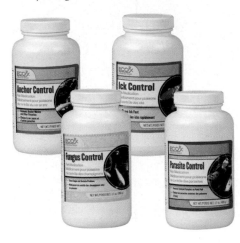

2. My fish are sick! What should I treat them with?

Don't treat with anything until (or unless) you have thoroughly ruled out deterioration of water quality. You should run tests for ammonia, nitrite, nitrate, and pH before deploying ANY remedy. This is because most cases of fish illness come from poor water quality.

3. My fish has white cottony stuff on it! What is that and how is it treated?

White cottony stuff could be any of three things. It could be bacterial infection, fungal infection, or epistylis. First, test your water, and then salt the water to 0.3% to clear epistylis. If the fish is valuable, bring it indoors, warm it gently, and feed it medicated food. This should clear bacterial or fungal infections smoothly.

4. Do I have to have a filter on the pond?

If you don't have many fish, or you don't feed very much at all, then you might not need a filter. However, any ornamental pond with fish living in it should have water movement to ensure gas exchange and oxygenation.

5. What kind of filter is the best?

The best filter is the one your neighbor (who doesn't even have to be an expert) still loves after two years. So ask around. There are many different kinds of filters on the market and they all work. However, they vary in terms of price, effort to maintain, and longevity. Therefore, get reliable testimonials from folks who've used the filtration you're considering for at least two years and still love them.

6. My pond has gravel on the bottom, and some people say it's bad. What should I do?

Don't do anything. Gravel on the pond bottom is not bad. What's bad is not cleaning that gravel every single year. Folks who perform the annual cleaning are happy with their ponds.

7. Are birds and frogs disease-carriers for my fish?

Under extreme conditions they can be. Birds and frogs can carry free form parasites on their plumage or on their skin. This is an extremely uncommon but suspected mode of transmission for certain pathogens.

photo by Robert Osler

8. Will salt kill my plants?

Yes. Just about any plant you hold dear or spent a lot of money on, will probably die when you apply salt. This is part of Murphy's Law. Remove any plant you really like.

9. Can koi and goldfish interbreed?

Yes, it happens accidentally as koi and goldfish are egg layers and they fertilize externally. The koi and goldfish hybrid is a large fish with a hump on its nape, and no barbells. The fish are usually earth colored, and they are universally sterile. They are hardier than either the koi or the goldfish.

10. How can I transport my fish?

Important rule: Fish should be transported under pure oxygen, in darkened coolers. All you need to do is get large, thick poly bags. Once you have a suitable bag, you can get an oxygen tank (sometimes by prescription) from your local medical supply place. Typical tank fees run from $18 to fill and $8 per month rent. Put the fish in the bag that is less than half full of pond water. You need more room for air than water. Drop in a water treatment tablet such as BagPrep™ and a pinch of salt. Close the bag around the oxygen tube and run oxygen into the water until the bag begins to get full of oxygen like a balloon. Let some pressure off and run the oxygen a few seconds longer. Don't make the bag 'tense' with oxygen, especially if the fish will be flying, or it will burst in the air. Then apply TWO rubber bands around the top of the bag to seal in the oxygen.

Place the bag in a cooler and off you go.

Under pure oxygen, perhaps with an ice pack under the bag, the fish can be expected to do well for up to 24 hours. Don't transport any fish in water over 80°F. If it's warmer than that, slip an ice pack under the bag before shipment or transport.

Closing Note

The most common mistake people make in regard to the health of their fish is overfeeding. There is no 'close second.' People love their fish, and they feed them almost constantly. This is a recipe for ecosystem (equilibrium) failure. The fish should be fed as sparingly as you can stand, perhaps only once per day. I feed twice per week in my water garden which is populated lightly with koi and goldfish. In my koi pond (which is just koi, just for koi), I feed once per day. Overfeeding contributes to overt, and occult pollution, and the health of the fish quickly deteriorates, ruining the experience of fish keeping.

Resources for fish health management

Books
Koi Health & Disease
Dr. Erik Johnson
Soft cover textbook. 160+ pages with 110+ images and step by step "how to" information, with detailed instructions about the different medications and how they're used.

Koi Health & Disease: The Technologies
Dr. Erik Johnson
Video in NTSC VHS format. This 120 minute video steps you through a basic fish health course, shows you all the common parasites, and describes and demonstrates the injection, anesthesia, microscopy, and other essential techniques of fish health management.

Fancy Goldfish
Rick Hess and Dr. Erik Johnson. Hardcover textbook from Weatherhill press. This full-color textbook gives you chapters on goldfish types, care, feeding, husbandry, and medicine. Images photographed by Fred Rosensweig.

Internet
There are numerous fish health and pond related resources on the Internet. Using Google.com you should be able to find any resource you need, but here are some highlights and places to start.

- **Koivet.com** – This was Dr. Johnson's first web site. It contains a decade of information, is searchable, and has a well-attended message forum for live chat and help. The site is 100% free.

- **Fishdoc.net** – Content by Dr. Erik Johnson and Frank Prince-Iles, of the UK. This site melds Frank Prince-Iles articles and teaching with a commonly asked questions forum and a searchable database for veterinary fish health talent near you. It's free, too.

- **KoiLab.com** – KoiLab.com is a fully funded facility where fish surgeries and other treatments are done in a clinical setting by Dr. Erik Johnson and recorded here for the benefit of the hobby. Illustrated.

- **KoiNews.com** – Soon to be the central hub of the hobby. To stay current on the latest treatment breakthroughs and developments, check out Koinews.com for updated information in all areas.

- **KoiCrisis.com** – Not library information, but this website contains genuine action items. This site attempts to guide a hobbyist through a sick fish outbreak, giving direction to an online study of the disease and treatments, which are refined to a pertinent recommendation that helps.

About the Author

Dr. Erik Johnson is a veterinarian, well known fish expert, and the author of several books on the subject of of koi and goldfish health. His book, "Koi Health and Disease" gives considerable detail in the areas of medications and how they are administered. For more details on these books which expand on the information given here, please visit KoivetBooks.com.

Dr. Johnson is a graduate of UGA and speaks and writes for national and international audiences. His fish laboratory can be visited online at www.KoiLab.com.

Chapter 7

Attracting Critters to Your Pond

and Keeping Them There

Y ou've got the water, you've got the plants, you've got the fish, but something just doesn't seem right in your aquatic paradise. Something seems to be missing … something that made every childhood vision of a lily pad complete. What natural ecosystem would be complete without cute little creatures who love to visit your pond?

Why Amphibians?

Well, besides being just plain cute, there's a valid reason why you would want frogs and other amphibians visiting your pond every year. They play important roles in the ecosystem. The number of amphibians in your pond can be a good indicator of its health.

A small, upper pond, separated by the main pond with a stream, is ideal for attracting tadpoles.

In fact, ecologists are constantly monitoring the frog population to make sure everything is running smoothly in nature.

Say So-Long to Harmful Insects

Amphibians are instrumental in keeping the undesirable insect population to a minimum. This is certainly a good thing for your neighboring garden, but is also great for those lazy summer nights when you want to sit on your deck and not have to worry about pesky bugs bothering you and your guests. Frogs and toads will keep the mosquito population in your yard at bay, and will also help with other annoying garden pests. Amphibians can be very handy when it comes to keeping slugs and rodents away as well. And what about those earwigs? Well, you can kiss them goodbye (if you want to get that close

to them) because a toad can eat over 1,000 earwigs each summer!

Having these wonderful creatures around reduces the need for harmful pesticides that conflict with Mother Nature! In fact, if you do decide to lure these wonderful creatures to your pond, it would be wise to stay away from fertilizers or pesticides that might harm them.

You may see certain species of salamanders by your pond as well.

Water Attracts

Almost any expert will admit that water attracts amphibians such as frogs, toads, salamanders, and newts. Mostly, these creatures flock to water because they need a place to breed and lay their eggs. Since tadpoles need water to live, it seems only natural that a pond is a great place to raise a frog or toad family.

Tadpoles and fish can be a deadly combination, however, because those tadpoles can be a great snack for your koi. Water features are often built with a place where the eggs can hatch and mature out of the reach of hungry koi. Something like a small, upper pond, separated from the main pond by a stream, would do the trick. Just make sure that the force of the waterfall doesn't push the eggs and tadpoles over the edge toward your fish and mechanical filtration system. The force of the pump inside the skimmer could pull your tadpoles straight into it. While tadpoles have been known to make it through the pump unharmed, it can be a wild, shocking ride for them.

Certain species of salamanders also need water in which to breed and raise their young (referred to as larvae). So, come breeding time, you may see these salamanders by your pond as well.

If you let areas of your garden grow wild, it will also provide a shady place for amphibians to relax and cool off.

Newts spend half of their lives in water and then, as adults, retreat to land. These part-time pond inhabitants have an interesting way of caring for their unborn. When the eggs are laid, the female wraps each sticky-coated egg in a leaf or other similar material using her hind legs. With as many as 600 eggs per year, it may take her as long as two months to produce her annual clutch.

Doing a Little More

Amphibians are complex creatures and need a little more than water to make your pond their permanent home.

Boggy Areas: Biologists suggest a boggy area full of native grasses and ferns to keep amphibians safe and happy in your yard. Local wetlands are great places to check out when looking to mimic the right environment for your little visitors.

Aquatic plants: Plants are very important because they provide food and shelter for both tadpoles and adults, and a breeding site for adults. Additionally, the native grasses planted beside your pond will grow to be tall and flowing, providing excellent shelter for your aquatic creatures. If you let areas of your garden grow wild, it will also provide a shady place for amphibians to relax and cool off.

It is very important that your pond get the right amount of sunlight and shade for your new inhabitants.

Permanent Shelter: A well-located rock pile can also lure toads, salamanders, and newts to your pond. They can be made out of, well, rocks, ... as well as bricks or broken concrete. The rock pile should receive both sun and shade, and where you put it depends largely on your climate. For example, if you live somewhere with hot summers, you'll want to put the pile in a mostly shady spot.

A "Toad"ally Bright Idea!

Some frog and toad lovers suggest using a light to draw these adorable creatures to your pond at night. Some people put lights up in their yard to accentuate their evening landscape or to keep animals away. For frog and toad enthusiasts, the exact opposite is true. The light should be set no more than three feet above ground, and placed near the garden.

photo by Sandy Gorney

clipart.com

As long as turtles have mud to burrow in, they will over-winter in your pond.

Insects are attracted to the light, giving your toads and frogs a great place to feed at night.

If You Build It, They Will Come ... and Stay

It is very important that your pond get the right amount of sunlight and shade for your new inhabitants. They need a little of both to keep their body temperatures in check. Since these critters love playing around in muck and debris, a perfectly manicured lawn is not their cup of tea. Letting your lawn grow a little longer than usual will give them a place to hide from predators while traveling from pond to pond. Leaving some tree, shrub, and garden litter out so that they have something to burrow through will help keep them safe as well.

Safety Is Key

While they need damp conditions, some frogs can actually drown in water.

photo by Mark Pastor

Remember, once they take a dip in the pond, you want to make sure they have a way out, and steep edges can be deadly to them. Make sure that your pond has shelves, complete with rocks and gravel, so there are no steep sides. A piece of driftwood set in a shallow portion of the pond can make a great dry resting spot for your favorite creatures too. If you have a larger pond, a floating platform anchored to something in the middle of the pond is a great idea. Salamanders and newts are especially fond of cool, damp spots under logs.

Be cautious when handling any of these creatures. Some species of amphibians have poison in their skin glands, which

can be harmful to you, your children, and your pets. Our touch can be a danger to them as well. The oils and lotions we have on our hands could harm them.

You Can't Lead a Frog to Water

It's great to want frogs, toads, and salamanders in your pond to complete an ecosystem, but you should be patient. Don't go to a store and purchase these animals to put into your pond. In many

In the wintertime, when ice forms over the surface of the pond, a hole must be kept open, allowing built-up gasses to escape.

places, it is illegal to release certain species into the wild because they could be detrimental to native plants and animals. Chances are that they will not stay at your pond anyway, and they may not survive in the wild. By no means do we suggest that you go to a local pond or wetland and catch these animals to bring back to your pond, either. It's not a good idea to remove them from their habitat because they will undoubtedly try to return to their place of origin and may be killed along the way.

Creating a Winter Wonderland

In the winter, frogs are attracted to water and they will even over-winter in your pond. Now, one of the myths out there is that frogs need to be in water that is at least six feet deep in

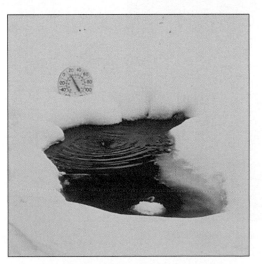

photo by Scott Hughes

The sound of running water is enough to make a bird curious to drop by.

order to hibernate. Not true! As long as you have mud for them to burrow in, whether it is a deep plant pocket or a potted plant, they'll be just fine. Make sure the pocket or pot is deep enough to keep them away from cold temperatures. If your pond is shelved, they'll probably go for the pot or pocket on the deepest shelf.

So, how do they keep from freezing? Simple. They are ectotherms, regulating their body temperatures largely by exchanging heat with their surroundings. The soil in the plant pocket or pot keeps the frogs nice and warm throughout the winter.

Like with fish, it is important to keep a hole open in the ice through the winter to circulate oxygen and allow harmful gases to escape. This can be done with a submerged, re-circulating pump bubbling at the water's surface, or combination of that and a floating de-icer. What you choose depends on just how cold it gets in your area. When the weather begins to warm up and it's time for the spring clean-out, gently wake them from their winter slumber.

Your Feathered Friends

Want to get birds to visit your backyard? Just add water! The sound of running water is enough to make a bird curious enough to stop on by. Once there, a nice cold drink or a refreshing bath will be their first priority, provided you keep a few things in mind.

Making Your Pond Bird-Friendly

Fresh, non-stagnant water during a dry summer is a must-have for the birds in your neighborhood, so why not be the gracious host that can provide them with a cool drink? A great rock or shallow stream will be a perfect spot for the winged-creatures to take a dip or a drink, without getting soaking wet. Slow moving water will also be a big attraction for birds, since a white-water experience is not what they're looking for when they land in your safe-haven!

If You Plant It, They Will Come

Native shrubs are perfect for around your pond and in your backyard if you are looking to attract birds. In essence, you are providing the birds with a habitat where they receive food and shelter, along with water. There are also a few other kinds of plants that will draw the birds to your pond and keep them there during the warm summer months, and sustain them through harsh winters.

Ornamental grasses, cosmos, zinnias, and asters are not only the perfect accent for your pond, they are also an abundant seed source for overwintering birds. Annuals like impatiens, larkspur, and nicotiana will also look great around your pond and attract your favorite birds. Foxglove, columbine, and coralbells are perennials that will bring birds your way. Cardinal flower, a plant that also attract birds, is especially fond

of water and can be planted in the shallow area at the edge of your pond.

Shrubs and trees will naturally draw birds for their berries, thick foliage, and strong branches. You must be aware that berries dropping from your shrub or tree into your pond will draw birds, but may also result in more upkeep for you.

Where there are plants, there are insects. Where there are insects, there are birds. Beetles, grubs, ants, worms, larvae, and other insects will make a great feast for your feathered friends when they come to visit your water garden. In fact, birds and plants are a great combination. Birds take care of plants by eating insects and destroying weeds, while plants take care of birds by providing food and shelter.

Get Ready!

It's always helpful to read up on any critters that you are trying to attract to your backyard paradise. So be sure to stop at the bookstore or library and pick up some reading materials on the subject. The more educated you are, the better off you'll be in the long run. Get ready! Once you get these creatures in your yard, you're never going to want to let them go! 🌿

For more information:
- Attract Reptiles and Amphibians to Your Yard, D. Cates, J. Olson and N. Allen, Oregon State University
- www.wildaboutgardening.org
- www.nwf.org
- www.floraforfauna.com.au

Chapter 8

Plants for Water Gardening Enthusiasts

Aquatic Plants

People who take the water gardening plunge come from a plethora of different backgrounds, and they're enticed into participation by a variety of different attractive features. But one of the most attractive features is the plant life that's inevitably associated with water gardening.

Being in the presence of the lush and aromatic plantings, from the water lilies and the lotus in the water, to the cattails, the iris, and mosses along the edge, to the infinite numbers of flowering, blooming, and blossoming terrestrial beauties surrounding the pond, is a compelling experience. It's an experience that makes you want to sit down, kick your feet up, clasp your hands behind your head, take a deep breath, and RELAX!

Water lettuce is a floating aquatic plant that can help starve algae in your pond. Its large, light green leaves grow in a rosette which resembles a head of lettuce.

Before you start planting, do a little research, ask questions, and learn about what you're about to plant.

What Happens if There Are no Plants?

Take those plants away and what do you have? Well, without going into detail, you don't have the same kind of experience described above. Yes, all by itself water has an attractive quality, but in order to make it feel natural, in order to transport you back into the belly of Mother Nature, to soothe and to relax your spirit to the max, plants are an absolute necessity in any well-conceived water garden. They also play an absolutely vital filtration role when it comes to having crystal clear water in your pond.

More Than Meets the Eye

By the same token, there's more to the planting aspect of water gardening than meets the eye. There are mistakes you can make that'll cause you headaches and work … the opposite of relaxation. There are some things that work better than others, given certain circumstances. When you're planning on building a new water garden and you want to make your new paradise all that you dreamed it would be, more knowledge is always better than less knowledge.

You'll Have Practical Knowledge

This chapter will give you enough practical knowledge about aquatic plants to cultivate a garden full of beautiful plants all by your lonesome. That's not to say that you'll know everything there is to know. That kind of knowledge grows and evolves from actual hands-on experience. However, if you understand the concepts discussed in this chapter, you will be ready to safely get your feet wet and avoid major mistakes that would cause you to have a problematic introduction into the plant world.

The lily – the most popular of the aquatic plants – has the ability to spread a multitude of leaves across the surface of the water and flower throughout the season. Lily pads provide a great deal of shade from the heat of the summer sun, allowing fish to retreat underneath the shelter of their leaves.

Water Lilies

A garden really isn't a "garden" without a plethora of plants. In the case of a water garden, the plants had better be aquatic plants. The very appearance of the words "water garden" should conjure up a colorful picture of a lushly planted aquatic landscape that's home to fish, frogs, and an abundance of other aquatic life. It's probably safe to say that one of the main reasons people enjoy water gardens is the beauty and unique characteristics of the aquatic plants that are a part of them.

The crown jewel of water gardens across the country is the lily. They are the most popular of the aquatic plants. Their ability to spread a multitude of leaves across the surface of the water and to flower throughout the season make them a sought-after addition to the pond. Lily pads provide a great deal of shade from the heat of the summer sun, allowing fish to retreat underneath the shelter of their leaves. They come in many different flower colors, shapes and sizes.

photo by Scott Hughes

flowers usually open in the early morning, and close by mid to late afternoon. When cold weather comes, the foliage dies and sinks to the bottom.

Tropical Lilies

Tropical lilies produce vibrant colorful blooms. The flowers, usually carried above the water surface on strong stems, come in brilliant whites, yellows, pinks, reds, and lilacs. Their leaves also come in an abundance of sizes, shapes, and colors. Tropical lilies, only hardy to zones 10 and 11 can be planted in colder zones when the water temperature is consistently above 70° F. Most tropical lilies are treated as annuals each year in colder climates. However, they can be brought inside and overwintered if given proper care.

Tropical lilies come in two categories, day bloomers and night bloomers. Day blooming tropical lilies bloom in the early morning and close in the afternoon. Night bloomers, however, begin to open in the late afternoon or early evening and continue to stay open until early the next

The colors range from yellow, pink, red, and white, with every shade imaginable from pale to vibrant, on the hardy varieties. If that's not enough, take a look at the tropical varieties and you'll find all shades of purples and blues, and even sunset orange. Even better, some tropical varieties will bloom during the darkness of night and come with a wonderful, heady fragrance.

You really can find a water lily to fit any need you may have. From growing it in a small container garden or a huge pond, from blazing sun to shade, from shallow water to deep, from night blooming or day blooming.

Hardy Lilies

Hardy lilies come in a wide array of colors, shapes, and sizes. They are reliably perennial from the northern reaches of zone 3 to the subtropical areas of zone 11 of the extreme southern United States. Refer to the hardiness zone map to find out which zone you live in before purchasing plants.

Each spring, new leaves will begin to arise from the submerged rhizomes and their stems soon begin to push the curled-up leaves to the surface of the pond.

The white, pink, red, or yellow flowers are often fragrant and known as the jewels of the water garden as they float on the surface. Hardy lilies typically bloom from May through September. Water lily

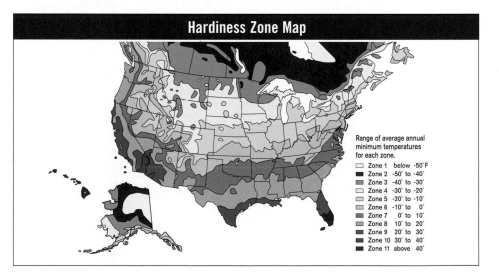

Hardiness Zone Map

Range of average annual minimum temperatures for each zone.

Zone 1   below -50°F
Zone 2   -50° to -40°
Zone 3   -40° to -30°
Zone 4   -30° to -20°
Zone 5   -20° to -10°
Zone 6   -10° to 0°
Zone 7   0° to 10°
Zone 8   10° to 20°
Zone 9   20° to 30°
Zone 10   30° to 40°
Zone 11   above 40°

photos.com

morning. For this reason, night bloomers are very appealing to pond owners who work by day and enjoy their pond by night.

Planting ... Pocket or Pot?

There are two basic methods of planting water lilies – the use of plant pockets, or aquatic plant pots without holes in the bottom. The method you use needs to be taken into consideration prior to pond construction. Whether you decide to plant the lily in a plant pocket or in a pot, the actual planting of the lily will be the same.

First, the size and location of the lilies must be determined. Water lilies will adjust their growth to the size of the area that they're planted in. So, size the plant pocket or pot according to the size of the pond. In most cases, a plant pocket should be 16-18" wide by 6" deep

or, if you choose to use an aquatic plant pot, it should be about 16" wide and 7" deep.

In a large pond, you may want the lilies to grow larger. Planting them in even larger plant pockets or pots will provide them with enough space to grow proportionate to the size of the pond. The size of the plant pocket, in this case, should be about 24" wide, or use a 24" wide by 10" tall aquatic pot.

If you prefer to use a plant pot, the hole should be just deep enough so the top of the pot is level with the bottom of the pond excavation. Allow a little extra room on the sides for folds in the liner. Ultimately, when the floor of the pond is graveled, it will have a flat, consistent appearance with no pots showing. If you are installing a water lily in an existing pond that does not have planting pockets, you will need to create a ring of rocks around the lily pot to hide it.

Constructing Lily Pockets

- **Lily pockets in an 11' x 16' pond**
  The typical 11' x 16' pond may have two or three lily pockets dug into the second shelf. The lily pockets are approximately 18" wide and 6-8" deep. Two or three pockets in an 11' x 16' pond will provide a healthy coverage of lily pads on the surface of the water.

- **Lily pockets in other areas**
  Don't feel limited to installing lily pockets on the second shelf only. Lilies have been known to grow in depths up to 15 inches. Take advantage of this by installing lily pockets in deeper portions of the pond. You can even dedicate entire shelves to lily pockets.

What if you failed to install lily pockets?

If you've already constructed the pond and left out the lily pockets, it's not too late. And, no ... you won't need to remove all of the rocks, gravel, and liner to install the pockets! Instead, build raised lily pockets inside the existing pond. These can be installed very easily while completing the annual pond clean out.

- Create the raised lily pocket using a ring of boulders.
- You will want to take measures to keep the planting soil from finding its way through the spaces in between the boulders. This can be accomplished either by using waterfall rock sealant or laying a small blanket of underlayment in the pocket to keep the soil contained.

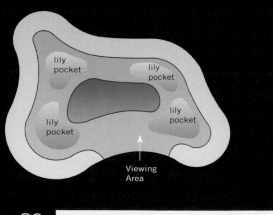

photos.com

Placement

Placement considerations are important too. Water lilies do not like heavy water movement or water splashing on their foliage, so they should not be located close to a waterfall or the base of a stream. Also, if a skimmer will be used, the lily should not be blocking the flow of water and debris into the skimmer.

Planting the Water Lily

After the liner is in place and the pond has been rocked, clean out any gravel that has fallen into the planting pocket. If you're using an aquatic pot, place the pot down into the hole you created for it and fill the area around the pot with gravel so the pot will not be visible.

If you're planting the lily directly in the pocket, fill it to within 1" of the top with heavy topsoil. Avoid using any type of potting soil that contains other added media, as it will float in the water. It's also important to make sure the soil has not been treated with any type of chemical that might harm the fish. In most cases, the topsoil that resulted from the pond excavation can be used.

Fertilizing

Fertilizing water lilies on a regular basis will encourage more frequent blooming and larger flowers. Time-released, granular fertilizer mixed

a granular, slow release fertilizer into the soil at the bottom of the plant pocket or pot and replant the largest clump with the crown at or just above the soil surface. A layer of pea gravel will keep the lily from floating away until it becomes established. (If you have koi, it's best to use a larger grade of gravel.) Cut off any ragged leaves and all the flower buds. The energy that would be spent blooming is better spent on growing roots right now.

into the soil at the bottom of the pot or plant pocket is a great way to fertilize lilies at the time of planting. Any other time, however, it would be messy and inconvenient. That's when lily fertilizer tablets work great. Whichever fertilizer you use, do not put it in direct contact with the plant's roots. The idea is to encourage root growth throughout the pot or pocket, so push tablets against the sides, away from the plant, and mix granular in only at the bottom of the pot or plant pockets.

Keeping Plants Healthy

To keep the plant healthy and the pond looking good, yellow or dead leaves, along with any spent flowers, should be removed on a regular basis. This will prevent them from sinking to the bottom of the pond and decomposing. Stems should always be pruned back as close to the base of the plant as possible.

Winter Care

Winter care of hardy water lilies is very simple. Fertilization should be stopped in the early fall as the growth of the plant slows. As leaves yellow, they should

continue to be removed, and after the first frost, 2/3 of the oldest foliage should be removed. The water lily will then go dormant in the bottom of the pond.

Tropical water lilies can be over-wintered however, it can be difficult and time-consuming. Some find they'd rather treat tropical lilies just like annuals and replace them each spring.

Dividing

Dividing lilies is an important part of maintaining beautiful and healthy plants. It's an easy and cost-effective way to get more lily plants for their pond or to share with fellow ponderers.

Clump-Forming Lilies

There are several types of water lilies, and becoming familiar with them is the first step in learning how to divide them. The clump form of a water lily will produce new, baby plants at the base of the mother plant. To divide, wash the soil off the roots and look for these delicate little plantlets at the crown, or growing point, of the larger plant.

Gently work them apart, cutting them, if needed, with a clean, sharp knife. Mix

Tuber-Type Lilies

This type of water lily produces new plants from it's potato-like tuber, which is a modified stem. Find a firm piece of the tuber with plenty of growth points and use a clean, sharp knife to cut off a section that is at least two inches long (three or four inches is better). It might be tempting to just snap off a chunk, but a clean cut will be less susceptible to fungal infection.

To avoid the spread of any fungal disease when cutting and dividing lilies, remove any mushy or discolored sections of the plant or tuber with a sharp knife and discard them. Be sure to clean your knife with a mild bleach solution before moving on to another plant!

In the End...

So, if there's a more popular aquatic plant on planet earth, it hasn't been found. It's water lilies ... and everything else is a complementary afterthought. Get the lilies right, and then work around them. If you do it that way, you'll have a happy, healthy, beautiful, and low maintenance water gardening experience.

Hardy Day-Blooming Lilies

Plant Name	Flower Color	Plant Size
Arc-en-ceil	Pink	Medium to large pond
Attraction	Red	Medium to large pond
Barbara Dobbins	Salmon	Medium to large pond
Berit Strawn	Changeable	Small to medium pond
Chromotella	Yellow	Medium to large pond
Chubby	White	Small to medium pond
Colorado	Salmon	Medium to large pond
Comanche	Changeable	Small to medium pond
Fire Opal	Pink	Small to medium pond
Gloire du Temple-sur-Lot	Pink	Medium to large pond
Gonnere	White	Medium to large pond
Helvola (pygmy)	Yellow	Container to small pond
Hermine	White	Small to medium pond
Indiana	Changeable	Small to medium pond
James Brydon	Red	Small to medium pond
Joey Tomocik	Yellow	Medium to large pond
Laydekeri Fulgens	Red	Medium to large pond
Lilypons	Pink	Medium to large pond
Perry's Baby Red	Red	Small to medium pond
Pink Beauty	Pink	Medium to large pond
Pink Grapefruit	Salmon	Medium to large pond
Red Spider	Red	Small to medium pond
Sioux	Changeable	Small to medium pond
Sultan	Red	Medium to large pond
Texas Dawn	Yellow	Medium to large pond
Virginalis	White	Medium to large pond

Tropical Day-Blooming Lilies

Plant Name	Flower Color	Plant Size
Afterglow	Sunset Orange	Medium to large
Albert Greenberg	Sunset Orange	Medium to large
Blue Beauty	Blue	Large
Carla's SonShine	Yellow	Medium to large
Crystal	White	Medium to large
Electra	Blue	Medium
Evelyn Randig	Pink	Medium to large
Jack Wood	Red	Medium to large
Judge Hitchcock	Blue	Large
Mr. Martin Randig	Red	Medium to large
Nora	Purple	Medium to large
Pamela	Blue	Large
Panama Pacific	Purple	Medium to large
Perry's Blue Heaven	Blue	Medium to large
Robert Strawn	Purple	Medium to large
Shirley Bryne	Pink	Medium
St. Louis Gold	Yellow	Medium to large
Tina	Purple	Medium
Yellow Dazzler	Yellow	Medium to large

Tropical Night-Blooming Lilies

Plant Name	Flower Color	Plant Size
Missouri	White	Large
Mrs Geo. Hitchcock	Pink	Medium to large
Red Cup	Red	Medium to large
Red Flare	Red	Medium to large
Texas Shell Pink	Pink	Large
Trudy Slocum	White	Large

A Visual Guide to Lilies

Attraction

Berit Strawn

Sultan

Red Spider

Pink Beauty

Comanche

Gloire du Temple-sur-Lot

Chromotella

Joey Tomocik

Virginalis

Hermine

Indiana

Laydekeri Fulgens

Perry's Baby Red

Arc-en-ceil

Carla's SonShine

Lotus

Lotus plants are a beautiful addition to any water garden. They come in a wide range of sizes — some varieties growing to 6-8' tall with leaves that are 18-36" in diameter. Smaller growing varieties only reach a height of 8-12" and have a leaf diameter of 2-3".

A Variety of Colors

There are many colors available. Pink, red, white, and yellow are the basics, but there are also many multi-colored varieties that combine these colors, as well as varieties that start out as one color, changing as the flower opens each day.

Construction Tips

When building the pond, make sure you create a shelf that is wide enough, and is excavated at the correct depth to accommodate the lotus. They prefer to grow in 4-8" of water. A plant pocket can be dug into the shelf to hide the aquatic pot, adding to the natural look of the pond.

Dividing

Lotus should be divided in the early spring as they first start to grow. This is done by un-potting the plant and gently pulling the long tubers loose from each other. You will find that they have wrapped themselves along the outside edge of the pot. The tubers look like a chain of white bananas. Find an end with a good growth point and go back two tubers and make a cut there. This will give you two growth points. One of these divisions is plenty for a 23" pot. If the tuber is soft, then it's no good and you should avoid using that portion.

photos.com

Planting

Lotus plants are best grown in pots, as they are extremely invasive if they're turned loose in a rock and gravel pond. Since they have a tendency to size themselves to the size of the container they are planted in, choose the size of container carefully. Lotuses, like water lilies, prefer a wide growing container. Most varieties can be grown in a 16 - 23" wide and 7 - 10" deep aquatic pot with no holes. Larger pots can be used in very large ponds.

To control the ultimate size of a lotus plant, a smaller pot should be used, but also pay attention to the variety you choose. Varieties like Momo Botan and Baby Doll can be grown in as small as an 8-inch aquatic pot. Larger varieties like Mrs. Perry Slocum or Resea Plena should be grown in a 23-inch aquatic pot. Make sure the size of the container is appropriate for the variety that you select.

To plant, fill the pot with 2 - 3" of heavy topsoil, placing the fertilizer tablets in the bottom (follow dosage recommendations on label). Make a small furrow in the soil and place the lotus tuber in it with the growth tip toward the center of the pot. Place a small rock on top of the tuber so it does not float, and cover the soil with a 1/2 to 1-inch layer of gravel. A lotus only needs to be repotted every two to three years, and by this time, the root system will have completely filled the container.

> *Lotus plants are best grown in pots, as they are extremely invasive if they're turned loose in a rock and gravel pond.*

Care

Lotus plants are hardy to zone 3 and can be found growing in most regions of North America. Due to their large leaves, they like a lot of sun and are heavy feeders. They should be heavily fertilized in the spring, then again at a lower rate as soon as flowers start to appear. In most parts of North America lotus will start blooming in mid-June to mid-July and continue into the fall.

And They're Cool Too!

One of the coolest things to do with lotus is to splash water onto the surface of the leaf, swish it around, and watch it bead and swirl around like droplets of mercury. Most people have never been exposed to this phenomenon and they tend to light up immediately when they see it. Lotus are graceful, colorful, beautiful, attractive to the eye, and even considered to be somewhat exotic in western cultures.

A Visual Guide to the Lotus

Mrs. Perry Slocum — Perry Slocum

President — Perry Slocum

Chawan Basu — Perry Slocum

Shiroman — Perry Slocum

Momo Botan — Perry Slocum

Maggie Belle Slocum — Perry Slocum

Lutea — Perry Slocum

Rosea Plena — Perry Slocum

Lotus Varieties

Plant Name	Color	Plant Size
Baby Doll	White	Small to medium
Charles Thomas	Med Pink	Medium to Large
Chawan Basu	White w/ red edge	Small to medium
Lutea	Pale Yellow	Large
Maggie Belle Slocum	Mauve Pink	Medium to Large
Momo Botan	Dbl Pink	Small to medium
Mrs. Perry Slocum	Red/Yellow	Large
Perrys Giant Sunburst	Yellow	Large
President	Red	Large
Red Russian	Red	Large
Rosea Plena	Dbl Pink	Large
Shiroman	Dbl White	Large

Marginal Aquatic Plants

Marginal plants are typically found along the perimeter of ponds, lakes, wetlands, and streams. These plants are used to soften the edges and help create a smooth transition from the water in the pond to the terrestrial planting area surrounding the pond. To create a natural-looking pond, a good selection of marginal plants is very important. There are hundreds of varieties to choose from and they come in all shapes, sizes, textures, and flower colors.

Most marginal plants prefer to be planted in 1-8" of water, so the first shelf in the pond, as well as the edges of streams and upper pools, are ideal planting areas. Any reputable aquatic plant dealer will have many varieties of marginal plants to choose from.

Attractive and Beneficial

Other than just adding beauty and naturalization, marginal plants also serve many other purposes in the water garden. They add valuable filtration to the pond and they remove elements that would otherwise feed algae. They attract and provide cover for wildlife. You can also select from among many different hardy or tropical varieties.

In a rock and gravel pond, marginal plants are generally placed directly into the gravel. This allows them to thrive naturally, and filter the water more effectively. Certain plants such as thalia, bulrush, and reeds can be problematic and may even damage the pond liner. For these plants, you should either avoid planting them altogether, or plant them in an aquatic pot to contain the roots. Surrounding the pots with rocks and gravel will help maintain the natural look of the pond.

Streams are another great place for marginal plants because they provide valuable mechanical filtration as the water flows past their roots. They also soak up additional nutrients, minimizing algae problems. Just picture the last time you saw a stream in nature and all the wonderful plants growing in the water along its edges. That's the look you want to create.

Planting Considerations

Start by selecting the proper plant for the water depth, sun exposure, and location. Water depth is an important consideration when it comes to choosing aquatic plants. More specifically, the concern is with how much water a plant will tolerate above its crown. For this reason, most marginals are planted on the first shelf of the pond. Select plants of different heights, foliage types, and flower colors to create a pleasing mix.

As you can see, shallow rooted plants can be planted almost anywhere.

After selecting the plants, it's time to place them in the pond. Start off by carefully washing away most of the soil from around the root system. Once the soil has been removed from the plant, push back the gravel and place the plant in the pond, filling the gravel back in around the root system.

The same process can be used for planting in a stream. Carefully select aquatic plants that like or tolerate the stream's moving water. Not all marginal plants can thrive in moving water.

Special Care for Aggressive Plants

If the plant you decide to use is overly aggressive, you should consider leaving it in a pot to help contain the spread of the roots. Remember, most aquatic plants prefer width over depth in their respective growing areas, so give them plenty of room to spread out by planting them in low, wide containers. Many marginals are shallow-rooted, therefore depth is less of a factor than surface area.

To plant, fill the holeless aquatic pot with 2-3" of heavy topsoil, placing the fertilizer in the bottom of the pot. Unlike the marginals you planted in the gravel, you will need to fertilize these plants as they are not as effective at drawing nutrients from the pond because their roots are contained by the pot.

Finish filling in around the plant's roots with heavy topsoil to 1" from the top, firmly pack the soil, and cover it with a 1/2-1" layer of gravel. When you're done, the gravel level should be about even with the previous soil level.

Maintenance

Taking care of marginal plants in a rock and gravel pond is fairly simple. Remove any dead, discolored, or excess plant material as needed. Marginal plants (unless they are in pots) do not need to be fertilized, as they will flourish from the nutrients in the pond.

For winter care, simply cut the plants back to 2-3" above the water level of the pond. In the spring, remove all dead plant material. And remember, the growth of plants that are directly in the gravel is not restricted – they will need to be thinned so they don't engulf more of the pond than originally planned.

On a Final Note…

The flowering water lily may be the apple of your water gardening eye, but marginal plants play a crucial role in the function, maintainability, and beauty of a properly-conceived water garden. Without marginal plants, the water garden will look out of place and un-natural. They provide many textures, colors, and blooms that soften the edges and help blend the pond into the surrounding landscape. So when you're in the planning stages of a water garden project, don't forget the marginals because they're simply part of Mother Nature's recipe … and we all know better than to argue with her.

Tip: Tropical marginal plants can be treated as annuals or brought indoors during cold periods. Some will survive cold spells if kept below the water's surface. We recommend planting tropical marginal plants in their pots. This will allow you to remove the tropical aquatics from the pond before winter approaches.

Marginal Plants

Plant Name	Scientific Name	Hardiness Zone	Height	Water Depth	Description
Arrow Arum	*Peltandra virginica*	4-10	24-30"	0-10"	Dark, glossy, green arrow-shaped foliage. Similar growth habit to a hosta. Sun to shade.
Bog Lily	*Crinum americium*	8-11	18-36"	moist-3"	Long-petalled, white flower with green strap-like leaves. Full to part sun.
Calla Lily	*Zantedeschia aethiopica*	9-10	12-24"	moist-3"	Dark green, arrow-shaped leaves with pure white, trumpet-shaped flowers.
Candy Stripe Reed	*Phragmites spp.*	5-11	48"	0-4"	Mint green foliage and canes are brightly striped with white and pink. Silver plumes in fall. Caution: Can be invasive, has been known to poke a hole in the pond liner, and if used, is best left in container. Full to part sun.
Canna 'African Sunset'	*Canna spp.*	9-11	30-40"	moist-3"	Variegated, dark purple foliage with orange-red flowers. Full to part sun.
Canna 'Bengal'	*Canna spp.*	8-10	48-72"	moist-10"	Brightly variegated leaves with cream, yellow, and green stripes, a subtle maroon edge, and large, orange flowers. Full to part sun.
Canna 'Black Knight'	*Canna glauca*	9-11	36-48"	moist-4"	Deep purple foliage with red flowers. Full to part sun.
Canna 'Endeavor'	*Canna glauca*	8-10	48-60"	moist-10"	A true aquatic canna with large, blue-green foliage and bright red flowers. Long bloom time. Full to part sun.
Canna 'Erebus'	*Canna glauca*	8-10	48-60"	moist-10"	Large blue-green foliage with soft, delicate peach-colored blooms. Long bloom time. Full to part sun.
Canna 'Florence Vaughn'	*Canna spp.*	9-11	48-72"	moist-10"	Flowers resemble giant gladiolas of orange with yellow edges. Full to part sun.
Canna 'Intrigue'	*Canna glauca*	8-10	36-60"	moist-4"	Beautiful, dark purple foliage with pinky-orange flowers. Full to part sun.
Canna 'Ra'	*Canna glauca*	8-10	48-60"	moist-10"	Large, blue-green foliage and bright yellow flowers. Long bloom time. Full to part sun.
Cardinal Flower, Queen Victoria	*Lobelia cardinalis 'Queen Victoria'*	5-9	24-36"	0-2"	With its wonderful deep burgundy foliage topped with red flowers, this plant is a great addition.
Cattail, Dwarf	*Typha minima*	3-10	12-36"	moist-4"	Thin, delicate leaves with small catkins, 1-3" long. Full to part sun.
Cattail, Variegated	*Typha latifolia 'Variegata'*	4-11	36-72"	1-6"	White and green variegation make this a wonderful addition to any pond. Full to part sun.
Chameleon Plant	*Houttynia cordata 'Chameleon'*	4-11	6-10"	0-2"	Multi-colored, heart-shaped foliage that is great for naturalizing. Full to part sun.
Forget-Me-Not	*Myosotis scorpoides*	3-9	2-6"	0-2"	Shallow, water plant with small blue flowers and velvety leaves. Full to part sun.
Golden Club	*Orontium aquaticum*	6-10	12-24"	0-6"	Waxy, green foliage with unique white and gold flowers rising above the foliage. Full sun to light shade.

Plant Name	Scientific Name	Hardiness Zone	Height	Water Depth	Description
Iris, Japanese	*Iris ensata*	3-10	24-36"	0-6"	These large flower irises beautify any water garden with a multitude of different colors.
Iris, Louisiana	*Iris spp.*	3-10	24-36"	0-6"	There are many different colors and varieties of Louisiana Iris: **Red** Bayou Rouge, Cherry, Bounce, Top Notch **Pink** Deneb, Handmaiden **Blue** Clyde, Redmond, Eolian, Mary Dunn **Yellow** Ila Nunn **Blue-Violet** King Creole, Marie Calliet **White** Winter's Veil, Acadian, White
Iris, Northern Blue Flag	*Iris versicolor*	3-7	24-36"	0-6"	Wonderful blue flowers in mid spring. Great for naturalizing and for wetland filters.
Iris, Siberian	*Iris siberica*	3-10	24-36"	2-4"	Siberian irises are one of the easiest and most reliable water irises to grow. They come in a rainbow of different colors.
Iris, Southern Blue Flag	*Iris virginica*	5-11	24-36"	0-6"	Wonderful blue flowers in mid spring. Great for naturalizing and wetland filters.
Iris, Yellow Flag	*Iris pseudocorus*	3-10	24-36"	0-12"	Brilliant yellow flowers in mid spring. Great plant for wetland filters.
Lemon Bacopa	*Bacopa caroliana*	7-11	2-4"	moist-2"	Lemon-scented groundcover with vivid, blue flowers. Full sun to shade.
Lizards Tail	*Saururus cernuus*	4-11	12-36"	0-6"	Long, foamy-white flowers spring to early summer. Very fragrant. Full to part sun.
Marsh Marigold	*Caltha palustris*	3-9	12-36"	0-2"	Mounding, native plant with round dark green leaves and bright golden-yellow flowers bloom in early spring. They don't like summer heat and grow best with some shade. Does best in zones 6 and northward. Part sun to shade.
Monkey Flower, Lavender	*Mimulus ringens*	5-11	20-30"	0-2"	Shiny, jade-green, upright foliage with lavender, snapdragon-like flowers in the summer. Grows better in gravel than in a pot. Full to part sun.
Monkey Flower, Yellow	*Mimulus guttatus*	5-9	12"	0-2"	Dense, light green, prostrate foliage with yellow, snapdragon-like flowers. Full to part sun.
Papyrus, Dwarf	*Cyperus isocladus*	8-10	24-30"	moist-4"	Like standard papyrus, but much smaller. Perfect for tub gardens. Full to part sun.
Papyrus, Egyptian	*Cyperus papyrus*	8-10	8'	moist-10"	Stiff, triangular stems tipped with ball-shaped clusters of needle-like leaves and flowers. Clumping plants have a gracefully, arching habit. Excellent accent plant. Full to part sun.
Parrot Feather	*Myriophyllum aquatica*	6-10	6"	0-3"	Feathery foliage floats on top of water or over edge of pond or pot. Full to part sun.

Plant Name	Scientific Name	Hardiness Zone	Height	Water Depth	Description
Pickerel Rush	*Pontederia cordata*	4-10	24-30"	0-10"	Shiny, green heart-shaped foliage with spikes of blue flowers. Also available in white, pink lavender, and tropical forms. Full to part sun.
Ribbon Grass, Strawberries and Cream	*Phalaris arundinacea* 'Feesey'	3-9	18-24"	0-3"	Pink, green, and white striped foliage during the spring, turning to cream and green during the summer months. Full to part sun.
Rush, Corkscrew	*Juncus effusus* 'Spiralis'	4-9	3-12"	0-2"	Twisting, tubular stems that resemble a corkscrew. Full to part sun.
Rush, Soft	*Juncus effuses*	4-9	24"	0-4"	Spiky, tubular stems makes a good filler plant. Full to part sun.
Siberian Pink Cups	*Baldellia ramunculoides f. repens*	2-7	2-10"	0-1"	Dense, pink flowers all summer. Great for stream or pond edge. Full to part sun.
Star Grass, Star Topped Sedge	*Dichromena colorata*	8-10	12-24"	moist-1"	Thin, needle-like stems with narrow leaves and white, star-shaped flowers. This native plant blooms all summer. Full to part sun.
Sweetflag, Variegated	*Acorus calamus* 'Variegatus'	5-9	30"	0-2"	Tall, clumping, iris-likc foliage with green and white stripes. Great for naturalizing. Attractive all summer. Full to part sun.
Sweetflag, Dwarf Variegated	*Acorus gramineus* 'Ogon'	6-11	8-12"	0-3"	Clumping, iris-like foliage with green and yellow stripes. Sun to part shade.
Taro, Black Magic	*Colocasia esculenta* 'Black Magic'	8-10	48"	moist-6"	Heart-shaped, burgundy-black leaves and stems. Makes a beautiful accent plant. Full to part sun.
Taro, Imperial	*Colocasia illustris*	8-10	48"	moist-6"	Large, heart-shaped, black leaves with green veins and edges. Striking plant is an excellent accent. Full to part sun.
Taro, Violet Stemmed	*Colocasia esculenta* 'Metalica'	8-10	48"	moist-6"	Large, velvety, green leaves with deep purple veins. Full to part sun.
Thalia, Powdery	*Thalia dealbata*	5-11	72"	4-12"	Oval, blue-green leaves that are edged in purple with small violet flowers. This hardy plant gives a tropical look to any pond. Sun to part shade.
Umbrella Palm	*Cyperus alternifolius*	8-10	48-60"	moist-6"	Very popular water garden plant. Stiff, upright, stems with narrow leaves arching from the top, resembling an umbrella. Tolerates some shade and moving water and is an excellent, natural filler plant. Full to part sun.
Water Bluebell	*Ruellia brittoniana*	9-11	24-48"	moist-6"	Tall, branching plant with deep purple flowers. Full to part sun.
Water Bluebell, Dwarf	*Ruellia brittoniana* 'Katie'	9-11	6-12"	moist-2"	Dwarf plant with deep purple flowers. Full to part sun.
Water Bluebell, Dwarf Pink	*Ruellia brittoniana* 'Pink Katie'	9-11	6-12"	moist-2"	Short, branching plant with medium pink flowers. Full to part sun.

Plant Name	Scientific Name	Hardiness Zone	Height	Water Depth	Description
Water Bluebell, Pink	*Ruellia brittoniana* 'Chi-Chi'	9-11	24-48"	moist-6"	Tall, branching plant with medium pink flowers. Full to part sun.
Yellow-eyed Grass	*Sisyrinchium californicum*	4-10	8"	2-3"	Short, iris-like foliage with bright yellow flowers. This plant will liven up the edge of any pond. Full to part sun.
Zebra Rush	*Scirpus lacustris spp.* taber 'Zebrinus'	4-9	24-48"	moist-6"	Tall, tubular, green stems with white banding that may fade during summer. A very popular accent plant for the pond. Can be invasive. Full to part sun.

A Visual Guide to Marginal Plants

Bog Lily — Eric Wood

Canna 'African Sunset' — Eric Wood

Iris, Southern Blue Flag — Doug Gilberg

Rush, Corkscrew — Doug Gilberg

Siberian Pink Cups — Eric Wood

Star Grass, Star Topped Sedge — Eric Wood

Pickerel Rush — Doug Gilberg

Ribbon Grass, Strawberries and Cream — Eric Wood

Taro, Imperial — Eric Wood

Thalia, Powdery — Doug Gilberg

Umbrella Palm — Eric Wood

Yellow-eyed Grass — Doug Gilberg

Floating Plants

Floating aquatic plants can be a very effective way of adding filtration and surface coverage to a water garden. Since these are free-floating plants (having no roots anchored in soil), they draw 100 percent of their nutrients directly from the water, feeding on nutrients that would otherwise feed algae.

Floating plants can be placed in the pond, but need to be situated out of the reach of the skimmer. Tucking floaters into the edges of the pond, or in and around lily pads, can help prevent the skimmer from drawing them in.

Helping With the Green

Heavy-feeding examples of floating plants are water hyacinth and water lettuce. These plants are great at helping a water gardener naturally discourage and starve algae, keeping the pond from turning green. The floaters also help by providing some shade, which, in addition to helping to prevent algae growth, also benefit the fish in the pond. Depriving algae of necessary sunshine is the best cure for a green pond.

Caring for floating plants is very simple. Keep them thinned back during the growing season and, in northern climates, remove them from the pond in the fall to prepare for winter. For ponds with skimmers, it's best to place floating plants in an area where they will not end up in the skimmer, blocking its opening. A good place to keep them is in the top of the biological filter, where all the nutrient-rich water will pass over their roots. It also helps to hide the opening to the filter.

Floating Plants

Plant Name	Scientific Name	Hardiness Zone	Description
Frogbit	*Limnobium spongia*	6-10	Fleshy, heart-shaped leaves growing in a 2-6" rosette. When crowded, the leaves will extend above the water surface; otherwise they lay flat on the water surface.
Water Hyacinth	*Eichhornia crassipes*	9-11	The most popular floater, with its succulent leaves and bright purple flowers – great at competing with algae for nutrients and light. It is illegal in many states due to its aggressive growth habit.
Water Lettuce	*Pistia stratiotes*	9-11	Large, light green leaves growing in a rosette that resembles a head of lettuce. Does best in part shade, but can be slowly acclimated to full sun. It may sunburn in some parts of the country.

They Could Be Illegal

On the other side of the coin, many floating plants can become aggressive because of their ability to absorb nutrients so well. It's easy to remove extra, unwanted plants in order to prevent an ecological takeover. Since there is no root system, it's a matter of simply pulling out the unwanted plants and throwing them in the compost bin.

Whatever you do, DO NOT throw the extras into any natural body of water. They can easily take over, and choke out native plant materials.

Because of their aggressive nature, many floaters are illegal in southern states. Before you use them in a water garden project, check with your local department of agriculture for your state's noxious weed list.

Submerged Plants

Submerged plants are often the most forgotten plants in a water garden, but they are one of the best plants for helping to balance the pond's ecology. They absorb nitrogen, provide shade, food, cover, and a spawning medium for the fish.

They are often referred to as oxygenators because they release oxygen into the water during the day. But, just like any other plant, they consume oxygen at night. Although, they are not capable of correcting an oxygen problem in a pond, these plants can help improve the health of a pond.

Hardy Oxygenating Plants

Because these plants are typically submersed, they generally don't grab the onlooker's attention like the lilies and marginal plants do. Oxygenators help reduce algae by directly competing for the same food source. Think of them as nutrient sponges. They also provide protection and coverage for small fish. They can be planted by simply pushing a bundle right into the gravel or sticking them around the edges of a lily pocket.

Floating-Leaved Aquatics

This category of aquatic plants is an in-betweener. These plants' roots are anchored into media of some kind, whether they're in plant pockets or pots, soil, or gravel. So they're not floaters. On the other hand, their leaves float on the surface of the water, but they're not lilies either.

Floating-leaved, or lily-like aquatics as they are also known, benefit the pond by soaking up the sunlight and nutrition that's available in the water, starving out

Submerged Plants

Cabomba

Canadian Pondweed

Hornwort

Plant Name	Scientific Name	Hardiness Zone	Description
Anacharis	*Egeria densa*	5-10	The most popular submerged plant with long branching stems and small narrow leaves.
Cabomba	*Cabomba caroliniana*	7	Cheery, green, segmented leaves grow at the bottom of the pond, anchored by the rocks. White flowers can sometimes be seen at the water's surface.
Canadian Pondweed	*Elodea canadensis*	3-9	A smaller, more compact, form of anacharis.
Eel Grass, Ribbon Grass	*Vallisneria spp.*	4-10	Tall, grass-like foliage, growing to a height of 24." Works great where there is current in the pond.
Hornwort	*Ceratophyllum demersum*	4-10	A non-rooting, submerged plant that has long stems covered with fine leaves.
Dwarf Sagittaria	*Sagittaria subulata*	4-10	A great plant growing only to the height of 2-5." When planted directly in the gravel, it can grow into a carpet on the bottom of the pond.

Submerged plants are one of the best plants for helping to balance the pond's ecology.

Lily-like Aquatic Plants

Snowflake

Water Hawthorne

©2003 clipart.com

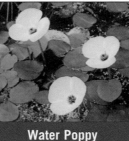

Water Poppy

algae blooms. They also provide shade for the fish in the pond, help oxygenate the water, and provide beauty and a diversity of plant life in the pond.

Many of these plants (including floaters, submerged plants, and floating-leaved aquatics) are tropical, and partial to the warm temperatures of zones 9 and 10. Often, they will also require protection during cold spells.

Plant Name	Scientific Name	Hardiness Zone	Height	Water Depth	Description
Water Hawthorne	*Aponogeton distachyus*	4-9	Surface Foliage	10-24"	Oval, green leaves float on the water surface with vanilla-scented, white flowers that open in fall and early spring. Usually goes dormant during the summer. Full sun to shade.
Water Poppy	*Hydrocleys nymphoides*	9-11	Surface Foliage	6-10"	Light yellow flowers and heart-shaped, shiny, deep-green foliage grow on stems that can trail by as much as three feet. Full sun.
Floating Heart	*Hydrocleys nymphoides*	5-10	Surface Foliage	12-24"	Round, glossy green leaves similar to that of a miniature water lily. Crepe paper-like, gold-yellow flowers are short-lived but plentiful. Can be invasive. Full-to-part sun.
Mosaic Plant	*Ludwiga sediodes*	9-10	Surface Foliage	12-24"	Beautiful rosettes of diamond shaped leaves. Does not grow well in water temperatures below 80°F. Full to part sun.
Snowflake	*Nymphiodes cristatum*	7-10	Surface Foliage	12-24"	Round, glossy, green leaves with red edges similar to that of a miniature water lily. White fringed flowers are short lived, but plentiful. Can be invasive. Full-to-part sun. Similar varieties: *N. hydrocharioides* (orange snowflake), *N. indica* 'Gigantica' (giant water snowflake).
Snowflake, Yellow	*Nymphoides geminate*	7-10	Surface Foliage	12-24"	Round, glossy green leaves with serrated edges. Snowflake-shaped, yellow, fringed flowers. Can be invasive in southern climates. Full to part sun.

Make sure that it looks really good from the most important view on the property.

Design and Plant Placement

Modern technology has made it possible for even the smallest urban lawn to be blessed with the presence of a water garden, complete with a waterfall! To ensure that your creation doesn't resemble modern technology, it's important to learn some of Mother Nature's aquatic design tricks. Landscaping the inside of a new water garden isn't much different than landscaping your backyard. In fact, the only difference is the type of plants.

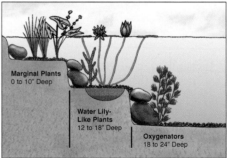

Marginal Plants
0 to 10" Deep

Water Lily-Like Plants
12 to 18" Deep

Oxygenators
18 to 24" Deep

Plant Placement Zones

Making It Natural

The addition of aquatic plants in the pond make it blend into the landscape, looking as though it occurred in the space naturally, rather than by human intervention. In nature, marginal plants are typically found along the perimeter of ponds, lakes, wetlands, and streams. In a man-made pondscape, these plants soften the hard edges of the rocks, and provide a smooth transition from the water in the pond to the terrestrial planting area that surrounds the pond.

The Best View

When you plan the aquatic or terrestrial plantings in and around your pond, you want to create maximum appreciation for the pond. Therefore, you should make sure that it looks really good from the most important view (the one with the highest traffic) on the property.

There are some basic ideas that might help you in your quest to imitate Mother Nature. First of all, remember that Mother Nature has no hands. Her style is guided by the wind. Taller marginal plants, placed as a backdrop, would naturally catch the flying seeds of other plants. The seeds would then drop to the bottom of the pond, and at least some of them would live again as a new plant where they landed.

When you're looking to mimic nature (with a little control), placing taller plants like reeds, cattails, and cannas near the back of a planting cluster works well. Then, add to the look by placing medium and shorter plants on the viewing side of the taller ones.

Playing With Colors

Random placement of plants with different textures and colors will give the pond a complete, yet unstructured, appearance. Choose the colors that you like best and let your creativity take care of the rest. It's always a good idea to emphasize primary colors with larger plants, and complete the look by adding some daring contrasts of texture and other colors around the edge.

It's easy to understand when someone says there are many different shades of green out there, but foliage comes in many other colors besides green. Getting creative with the colors and textures of foliage will help create a lush and inviting look.

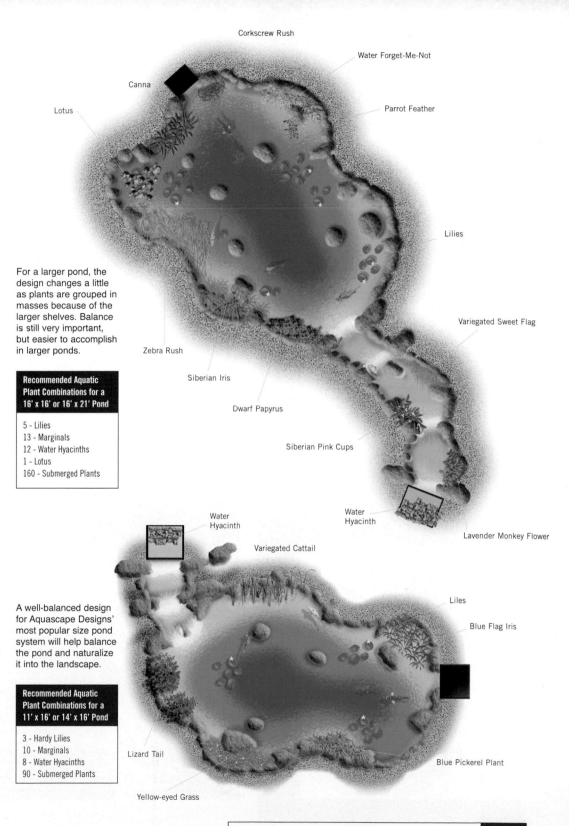

For a larger pond, the design changes a little as plants are grouped in masses because of the larger shelves. Balance is still very important, but easier to accomplish in larger ponds.

Recommended Aquatic Plant Combinations for a 16' x 16' or 16' x 21' Pond

5 - Lilies
13 - Marginals
12 - Water Hyacinths
1 - Lotus
160 - Submerged Plants

A well-balanced design for Aquascape Designs' most popular size pond system will help balance the pond and naturalize it into the landscape.

Recommended Aquatic Plant Combinations for a 11' x 16' or 14' x 16' Pond

3 - Hardy Lilies
10 - Marginals
8 - Water Hyacinths
90 - Submerged Plants

How to Plant Aquatics

With just a few exceptions, you can lose the pots to make your pond look more natural. Aquatic plants will help filter the water and reduce algae however, they will be far more successful at doing so if they are taken out of their pots and planted directly into the gravel substrate. Once planted, the roots will make their way through the gravel, sometimes as far as two to three feet away from the base of the plant. The roots then become one giant filter that takes nutrients directly from the bottom of the pond, where fish waste and other organic debris settle and begin to decompose.

Water lily Rhizome

Flowers, and the multitude of colors they come in, make easy work of naturalizing the water garden canvas, much like Monet and Degas mixed the various dots of color in order to bring the canvas to life — to make it shimmer in the eye of the beholder. You should aim to create something very similar with the various colors of your water gardening plants.

The Height Factor

It's important to be familiar with the mature size and habit of the plants that you include in your plan. Since you don't want to hide the shorter plants by placing them behind taller ones, it's important that you place the shorter plants in the foreground and gradually work your way back to the taller ones. It's much like how a photographer lines up a group of people in order to get all faces in the photo. In this case, you want to get all the faces of the plants in view.

One of the biggest mistakes that people make when planting a water garden is failing to realize how large some plants will grow or spread. When this mistake is made, the result is an overgrown "jungle" look that will require much more work to keep these plants from taking over the pond. In other words, if you want to create a truly low-maintenance water garden, have a pretty good idea of how large a plant is going to grow before you put it in the pond. When you actually do the planting, give the plant sufficient room to grow. In summary, the more fully you take all of these factors into consideration when designing and planting a water garden, the better the results will be.

How to Plant Hardy Lilies

Lily pockets should be dug during the excavation of the pond. The easiest time to plant lilies is when the pond is empty.

Planting Potted Lilies into "Soil-less" Lily Pockets

If your aquatic plant supplier provides the lilies already potted, then you will not want to add soil to the lily pockets. In this case, simply use the soil that the lily comes planted in.

1. Remove the lily from the pot.

2. Place the lily into the lily pocket.

3. Loose gravel should be spread around the base of the lily to prevent the soil from being stirred up in the pond.

Planting Bare-Root Lilies into "Soil-filled" Lily Pockets

You may want to prepare the lily pocket ahead of time by filling it with soil. This is especially efficient if your aquatic plant supplier sells lilies bare root or you're not able to plant the lilies at the time of construction.

1. You may want to prepare the pocket first.

2. Bare-root lilies can be planted directly into the soil-filled plant pocket.

3. Use commercial aquatic plant soil to fill the plant pockets prior to planting. Ask your local plant supplier for more information on commercial aquatic soils.

4. Place the lily tuber into the soil.

5. Loose gravel should be spread around the base of the lily to prevent the soil from being stirred up in the pond.

6. Ready for water!

How to Plant Marginal Plants

Marginal plants can be placed anywhere along the first shelf of the pond (0-8" deep areas), and also along the stream edges and upper pools.

1. Simply create pockets and crevices in between the boulders for easy marginal planting.

2. When ready to place marginal plants, simply choose the area and move the gravel aside with your hands. Remove the marginal plant from the pot.

3. Place the plant into the desired planting area.

4. Spread the gravel around the base of the plants.

The layout for marginal plants can be put into place while setting rocks and boulders. You can even take a similiar approach to lily pockets and create specific areas on your first shelf that contain soil. (see photo above) Smaller boulders and additional gravel can be used around the base of the plant to support it until the roots take hold.

How to Plant Floating Plants

Larger floaters, such as water hyacinth and water lettuce, do a great job of disguising the open top of the BIOFALLS® (biological) filter, as well as providing excellent filtration.

1. Place floating plants inside the BIOFALLS® filter. This keeps plants from spreading and hides the BIOFALLS® filter.

2. Set a green bamboo planting stick, or tie a monoflament fishing line, across the face of the BIOFALLS® filter to prevent the flow of water from carrying them over the filter.

3. Large floating plants can also be placed out of reach of the skimmer by tucking them behind the lily pads, such as these water hyacinths.

How to Plant Tropical Lilies

You may want to keep tropical lilies in containers if you plan on overwintering them. It's also a good idea to keep overly aggressive plants, such as lotus, in their container to prevent them from uncontrollably spreading through the pond.

1. Prepare a pocket for the pot with a ring of rocks.

2. Lower plant and pot into rock pocket.

3. Adjust rocks around pot as necessary to hold it in place.

4. Pot, plant, and rocks are ready for water.

Now You Know What You Need to Know...

You now have a basic, general, and practical sense of what works and what doesn't work when it comes to plants in and around your water garden. Although this knowledge will serve as a parameter, all water gardens are highly personalized creations, and yours will be too. When it comes to planting your pond, don't forget to bring your imagination along for the ride, and have a wonderful time in your very own, plant filled, aquatic paradise. 🍃

Chapter 9

Rocks and Gravel

Rockin' in the Pond

Other than water, the main components in a well-designed water feature are rocks and gravel. They're used to naturalize the feature, create waterfalls, and increase the biological activity in and around the entire pond. Simply put, rocks create a natural feel for the entire water garden.

Good Reasons for Gravel

There are many purposes for using gravel on the horizontal surfaces of a water garden. First, gravel serves as a cost-effective sun block that prohibits ultra violet rays (a rubber liner's worst enemy) from attacking the rubber liner. This, in turn, increases the liner's longevity and decreases maintenance time and cost.

Gravel also lends structural stability to the pond. To achieve this, gravel is placed in between and behind the boulders, eliminating the spaces between them and keeping them from shifting around. The gravel becomes a free-floating mortar, naturally locking the boulders into place.

It Holds the Liner in Place

Next, the sheer weight of the rocks and gravel help keep the liner in place and prevent it from moving once it's set. If you don't use them, the liner can even get air bubbles from underneath, and on occasion, it has even been seen bubbling up over the surface of the pond. If you've nicknamed your pond "Loch Ness," that bubbling effect may be a welcome sight; however, for most pond owners, it would cause panic and frustration.

Prevents the Banana Peel Effect ... You Slipping

You see, many people like to get in their pond on a hot day, after a run, a walk, or an hour of working in the garden. Step into a pond without rocks and gravel on the bottom, and your odds of slipping on the liner are increased dramatically. If you do put rocks and gravel on the bottom of your pond, you'll enjoy injury-free pondering experiences for years to come.

Which Gravel to Use?

The best gravel to use is similar in character and color to granite boulders, only smaller. The gravel is smooth, giving it a water-worn feeling that's easy on the feet, for those who venture into their pond.

Chapter 9 - Rocks and Gravel

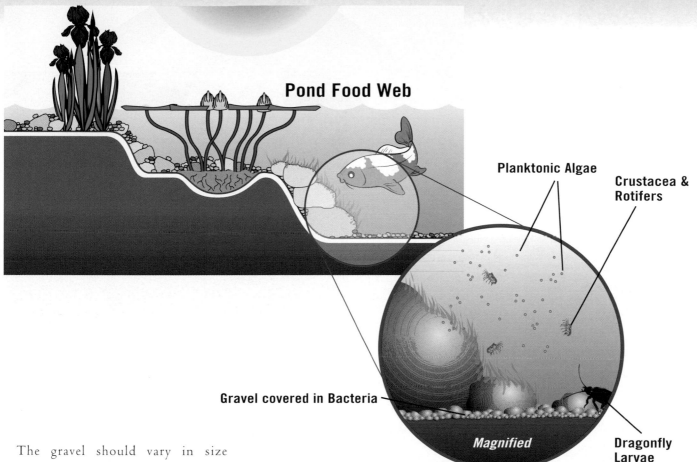

Pond Food Web

Planktonic Algae

Crustacea & Rotifers

Gravel covered in Bacteria

Dragonfly Larvae

Magnified

The gravel should vary in size to create a more natural appearance. The larger pieces give mass to the gravel bed and act as a nice transition to the larger boulders. The smaller sizes give you plenty of surface area, which is key for the pond's biological activity. Most stone yards will mix multiple sizes (3/8" up to 3") for you.

How Gravel Helps the Ecosystem

Providing a habitat for beneficial microorganisms is another reason for having gravel in your pond. The rocky bottom is totally alive and brimming with activity. It is covered in algae, microscopic invertebrates, and bacteria. This section of the pond is basically a compost pile.

Fortunately, nature has given us an easy way to solve this problem. Organisms have evolved to use practically every bit of available food. Fish, crustaceans, and aquatic insects will feed on these minute organisms, as well as bacteria and algae that live on the rocky pond floor.

This bacteria helps break down the decaying plant matter and fish waste, turning it into usable plant nutrition, which is then consumed by the aquatic plants over and over again in the aquatic "circle of life." Without the rocks and gravel, the bacteria would not thrive and the decaying plant matter and fish waste would accumulate on the pond bottom, getting deeper and deeper. This is the muck that you slip on if you've ever walked in a pond without rocks and gravel. Talk about noxious gasses! Far less of this muck is able to accumulate when you have rocks and gravel in a pond.

> *Without the rocks and gravel, the bacteria would not thrive and the decaying plant matter and fish waste would accumulate on the pond bottom.*

The Types of Stone Available

There are many types of stone available on the market.

• **Granite** – This is a common stone, frequently used in the Midwest for all types of construction – including home building, landscaping, and water features. Granite is a hard, crystalline rock that consists of feldspar and quartz. It's found in two forms, rounded cobblestones or boulders, and quarried chunks blasted out of large granite deposits. Granite

is inert, meaning it will not leach any minerals into the water. This, of course, means it's beneficial to pond building. Granite boulders come in a wide range of sizes and colors, making them easy to work with. They look best when set in a random, naturalistic manner.

Granite

• **Aqua-Blue Boulders** – This stone is great for water features. It is often used because of its rustic beauty and character. Aqua-Blue is a gneiss-based stone, meaning it is very similar to granite but has a bluish gray coloring and is considerably heavier than regular granite. These stones are harvested from natural hillsides, or quarried. The harvested stones are more interesting because they've been weathered and may have

Aqua-Blue Boulders

mosses and lichens growing on them. Their rustic character allows them to be placed as accents throughout a property, or used as focal points in a pond or waterfall.

• **Fieldstone** – This type of stone is found in local fields. The term describes many different types of rock, depending on what part of the country you're in. This is typically an inexpensive stone because of its local availability. In many instances, it may be the material of choice and it makes a good filler stone on the bottom of large ponds where it will never be seen. Be careful with fieldstone, however, because it may be a soft, limestone-based stone that can alter the water chemistry. If you're unsure, you can test the stone by pouring vinegar

Fieldstone

over it. If it foams and bubbles, it's limestone.

• **Moss Rock** – This an aged and weathered stone of various origins that has mosses and lichens growing on it. It's typically a sedimentary stone, and somewhat porous. It's considered to be

Moss Rock

a character stone and can be quite expensive, depending on your location. This is a highly sought-after stone because when it's used in and around a pond or stream, it will give the pond a sense of age, even though it may be a new pond.

- **Limestone** is a sedimentary rock composed mainly of calcium carbonate. Typically, it's a flat stone that's used in patios and walls. Larger pieces are

Limestone

used as landscaping outcroppings. For many years, it was a staple of waterfall construction because of its availability and ease of installation. You basically stack it up like a staircase and with very little imagination, it will still usually look nice. This type of stone should be used sparingly in a pond because the calcium carbonate will alter the water chemistry, which can lead to problems such as increased algae growth.

Basalt

- **Basalt** is a heavy, dark, volcanic rock. It is relatively easy to use and when obtained locally, can be inexpensive. The broken pieces can be fit together like a giant puzzle. The dark color hides water stains, and does not leach minerals into the water.

How Much Stone Do You Need?

Now you'd like to know just how much stone to order for your water garden project, right? Here, we'll show you how to calculate, for example, the rocks needed for an 11' x 16' pond with a medium waterfall and a 20-foot stream. Here is the formula that Aquascape Designs has used to build hundreds of ponds all over the country.

Boulders:
- In the Pond
  - Formula: Length in feet x width in feet / 40.
  - Example: 11 x 16 = 176 / 40 = 4.4. Round up to 4 ½ or 5 tons to be safe.
  - Tip: For a more natural look, use an assortment of sizes. Aquascape recommends a mixture of 6 to 12" and 12 to 18" granite boulders. For a really great effect, you can include about a ½ ton of 18 to 36" boulders to set into the edge of the pond. These make great sitting stones for feeding your fish.
- In the Stream
  - Formula: 1 ½ tons of boulders for every 10' of stream length.
  - Example: The stream that leads from your waterfall to your pond is 20' long, you would need 3 tons of boulders.
  - Tip: For a great assortment of sizes, use a 1:2:1 ratio of 6 to 12", 12 to 18", and 18-24" boulders. The larger stones will be used to naturalize the edge of the stream.
- For the Waterfall
  - Formula: Small Waterfall = 1 ton of assorted boulders, Medium Waterfall = 1 ½ tons of assorted boulders, Large Waterfall = 2 to 3 tons of assorted boulders.
  - Example: Your pond has a medium waterfall, so you'll need 1 ½ tons of boulders.
  - Tip: Framing the waterfall with larger boulders will help create a natural-looking cascade of water.

Gravel:
- In the Pond
  - Formula: 30% of the total quantity of pond boulders.
  - Example: Your pond contains 4.4 tons of boulders, so you would need 1.32 tons of gravel.
  - Tip: Ask your rock yard for a mixture of assorted sizes ranging from ½ to 3" gravel. This serves a number of purposes, including prevention of compaction and flexibility of filling gaps in the larger rocks.
- In the Stream
  - Formula: 30% of the total quantity of stream boulders.
  - Example: Your stream contains 3 tons of boulders, so you would need .9 tons of gravel.
  - Tip: Ask your rock yard for a mixture of assorted sizes ranging from ½ to 3" gravel. This serves a number of purposes, including prevention of compaction and flexibility of filling gaps in the larger rocks.

When rocking the pond, start on the bottom of the pond to keep the liner from being stretched too tightly as you work your way through the pond.

Getting to Know the Stone

There are many other types of stone, but most of them can fit into one of the above categories. For more detailed information on this subject, talk to your local rock supplier. If there is a certain stone you would like to use, let your dealer know and, depending on the quantities, he may be able to get it for you. Remember, the main goal is to create a naturalistic water garden and waterfall.

When ordering stone for a standard project, you should use a ratio of 1:2:1. In other words, order one part small (6-12") stone, two parts medium (12-18") stone, and one part large (18-24") stone. This gives you, the designer, a

The gravel becomes a free-floating mortar, naturally locking the boulders into place.

good variety of rock to work with for the project.

A Simple Stone Setting System

Start with the lower shelf:

- Always start on the bottom with some extra slack in the liner. This keeps the liner from being stretched too tightly as you work your way through the pond.
- Set the larger character stones first, and then fill between them with medium and small stones.
- Unless the pond is large, stones larger than 18" should not be used because they take up too much room in the water garden

The middle shelf:

- Use a good mix of rock sizes, with one or two large stones possibly sticking up out of the water, creating a rocky island.

The top ledge:

- This is where the most care should be taken because it represents the

What If a Stone Doesn't Fit?

If a large stone doesn't fit, you can adjust the excavation as needed. That's the beauty of using a liner instead of concrete or a preform. It's easy to make a change or adjustment, even after the liner has been installed.

To make an adjustment:
- Set the desired rock in place. **(A)**
- Mark the area behind the rock with a shovel.
- Move the rock out of the way. **(B)**
- Move the underlayment and liner out of the way, then dig the area out according to the shape of the rock. **(C & D)**
- Put the liner, underlayment, and rock back in position. **(E & F)**

It's that easy, and it gives the pond edge a clean, customized look. The entire pond perimeter can be done this way, but it can be very time consuming. It's all up to you, your creativity, your time, and the strength of your back!

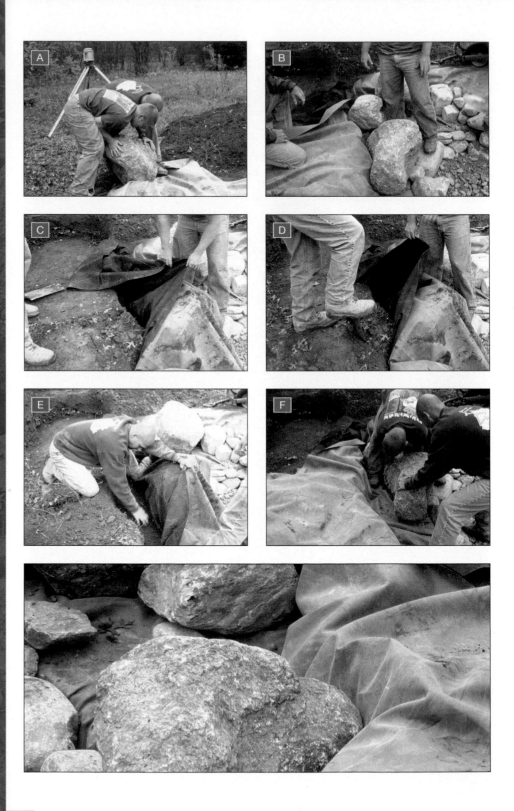

greatest amount of shoreline, which equates to the greatest amount of stone, and therefore, the greatest amount of required time.

- It's also the area that everyone will be looking at, so you want to be sure it looks good.
- Accentuate curves that have been excavated into the top ledge by placing larger stones on the inside curves of the pond, or where a peninsula juts into the water.

When constructing a water feature, you should use various sizes of boulders. Because your rocks vary in size, just like in nature, you should fill the spaces between with various sized gravel. When the cracks are filled, the gravel acts as a dry mortar, locking everything into place.

A Stony Controversy

The hobby of water gardening, as it has developed over the past decade, is full of technology and innovation. Now this low maintenance hobby is appealing to more and more hobbyists than ever before. Unfortunately, it's a hobby that can be full of misinformation which is left over from years gone by, before the new technology and the innovations were developed.

They Mean Well

The problem is aggravated still further when innocent people actually read the misinformation, act on it, and proceed to have miserable water gardening experiences. Then they turn around and share their bad news with other would-be water gardeners.

Reality Check

Now, if any of these well-intended advice givers had actual hands-on experience with rocked and graveled ponds, they'd know these things already and they'd cease dispersing "theories" which simply fail the reality test in modern water gardening.

Learn from Experience

The best way to get real answers is to check with anyone who has a rock and gravel lined pond in their yard. Ask them to tell you about their own personal experiences with their gravel bottomed ponds. Then, just sit back and listen. After you've had this conversation, you will probably chuckle over what you've heard in the past, and the kind of foolishness that is passed off as "information."

From Theory to Practical

One of the biggest and most controversial pieces of misinformation that still haunts the water gardening hobby, is the claim that rocks and gravel on the bottom of a pond are detrimental to it. The fact is, the significant sludge buildup on the bottom of a pond is greatly decreased by the use of rocks and gravel.

This concept works in an aquarium, so why wouldn't it work in a pond? Besides, the addition of rocks and gravel just makes the pond look more natural than a visible liner.

- The outside curves, or coves, of the pond, are lined with smaller stones. This is also where the aquatic plants can later be placed.
- The key is to spread the stone out, giving it a balanced, free-flowing feeling.

What About a Pre-Formed Pond?

What if you just bought a pre-formed pond and they told you to avoid rocks and gravel? What then? In this instance, Mother Nature will have to give way to technology because rocks and gravel in a plastic tub will only beat it up and create problems. You will want to make sure you have a biological filter where the desirable aerobic bacteria can colonize. It will also stick to the walls of the liner and that helps minimize the presence of ... algae.

The recommended thickness of the gravel layer running along the bottom of the pond is no more than two inches. Exceeding two inches presents the possibility of causing the accumulation of slime and muck which can affect the quality of the water and can cause your fish to experience problems.

One Final Note

If you're installing a rubber-lined pond then, for a variety of reasons, rocks and gravel are a must. But if you're installing a plastic, preformed pond, you'll just have to live with less surface area on which the aerobic bacteria can colonize. In the end, you'll know if you made the right choice by visibly detecting the amount of green in your pond. 🍃

Chapter 10

Water Gardens and the Environment

What is an Ecosystem Anyway?

Stop!!! Look no further; you've finally found it... Step-by-step ecology. Anyone who owns a pond has probably attempted to read books and articles on ecology, just to get lost in the scientific mumbo jumbo.

Let's Start From the Very Beginning...

The word ecology comes from the combination of two Greek words (oilcos, meaning house) and (logos, meaning study of). Together it literally means "study of the home." In the big picture, it's hard to comprehend all the inter-woven intricacies of a global ecology. Consider this example: Joe has been speaking about his inability to attract songbirds to his house, despite the

It takes time for animals to find a good habitat, but eventually, they will come.

fact that he puts birdseed out daily. It is only eaten by blackbirds. In order to resolve this problem, Joe buys a book on songbirds.

The book informs him that songbirds feed on a variety of seeds, berries, and insects. They also require water, shelter from predators, and a place to nest.

Joe's backyard is like the many others in suburban America. There is one tree and a sea of grass. Okay, this makes sense. He can't get birds here because he is only providing one of the many daily requirements of the songbirds. Joe needs to recreate the natural habitat in which songbirds live.

All this is starting to make sense to Joe. So, using the information in his bird book, he makes a list of plants: sunflowers, asters, cornflowers, black-eyed susans, a serviceberry, viburnum and bayberry.

Joe doesn't consider himself a "green-thumb" so he goes to the local garden center to get more information on the plants that he wants to grow. The store manager gives Joe a quick lesson in horticulture, explaining the importance of soil preparation, watering, and sun tolerances, so the plants he has purchased will thrive.

With his newfound knowledge of plants, Joe hurries home to start digging. He follows the planting instructions carefully, and he's thrilled with the outcome. A week goes by, and there are still no songbirds. *Joe realizes that it takes time for animals to find a good habitat, but eventually, they will come.*

In the meantime, Joe continues to read about songbirds and discovers that some of them like to forage for insects in compost and leaf litter. Joe normally has his yard waste hauled away, but now, he figures he should give composting a try.

He starts a compost pile of lawn clippings, leaves, and small twigs. The pile of decomposing organic matter is the perfect home for worms, millipedes, and springtails. The insects feed off of the organic matter, and birds feed on the abundant insect life. The by-product of the compost pile is a valuable soil amendment, full of nutrients for Joe's bird garden. Joe has established a miniature food web in his own backyard. From his love of birds, Joe has learned to love the plants that feed the birds, the soil that feeds the plants, and the insects and minute organisms that enrich the soil and feed the birds. Now, that's a lesson in ecology. It's all about the relationships among the various dimensions of Mother Nature, and how they work together to form a home … the one we generally call planet Earth.

Ponds Are a Piece of the Ecological Puzzle

Remember, the word ecology comes from the Greek words meaning "study of the home." Understanding pond ecology is just like Joe's understanding of songbirds. Everything has an impact on, or is impacted by, a pond in your backyard.

Ponds are one of the most important ecosystems on the planet. They play host to a total interrelationship of all organisms in the environment such as birds, fish, frogs, plants, and many microscopic organisms. So, ponds not only create a natural ecosystem in their defined environment, but they also fit into the community or life cycle of the entire ecological region. Now, that's cool!

An ecological region is made up of thousands of elements. Water is the most basic of these. Each pond is a piece of the puzzle. As wild habitats are depleted due to commercial development and other factors, these pieces are eliminated. That is why it's so important to restore and preserve as many of these "puzzle pieces" as possible. A backyard pond restores part of an ecosystem. So, don't view your pond as an individual, independent, or unrelated element. See it instead as part of the big picture, the regional environment.

A regional ecosystem or a pond ecosystem is like a triangle. In a regional ecosystem, ponds, streams, and lakes (water) are the support, like the base of a triangle. In the pond ecosystem, the water is the base of the triangle. Everything found above the base is completely dependent, either directly or indirectly, on the pond. Since water is at the base of all these diverse forms of life, it's important to understand some of its properties.

An ecological region is made up of thousands of elements, and each pond is a piece of the puzzle.

Typical ponds have a pH range between 6 and 11, which is slightly acidic to strongly basic.

Water Quality

A Mini Lesson on pH

pH stands for potential of hydrogen. The pH scale represents the relation of hydrogen ions to hydroxyl ions. Higher hydrogen content equals more acidic water, and as hydroxyl ions outnumber hydrogen ions, the water becomes more basic. pH is measured on a numbered scale of 1-14. A pH of 7 is neutral. This means that the hydrogen and hydroxyl ions are in complete balance. Numbers above this are called basic or alkaline. A pH below 7 is termed acidic.

Typical ponds have a pH range between 6 and 11, which is slightly acidic to strongly basic. For instance, 8.2 would be a very acceptable pH level. A pH of 4 is strong enough to dissolve nails so, needless to say, this is not good for aquatic life.

There are many things that influence the pH values in water. Probably the most influential are existing dissolved minerals and metals found in the water. These elements are buffers, typically expressed as alkalinity and hardness.

Helpful Tip: The pH levels in a pond involve many variables. This makes it very difficult, and potentially dangerous, to use chemicals to change the pond's pH levels. If you have hard water, chances are that even large quantities of chemicals won't immediately change the pH. They may cause the pH to suddenly and drastically drop, making your whole system crash.

- Alkalinity-The higher the alkalinity levels the more the water becomes "stuck" at a higher pH. Alkalinity is made up of the total of all buffering elements in the water typically expressed in ppm (parts per million).
- Hardness- Refers to the amount of dissolved calcium and magnesium or CACO3 in the water. Water is termed "hard" when levels are around 300ppm or more. The higher the hardness and alkalinity values, the lower the chances that you will have fluctuations in your pH.

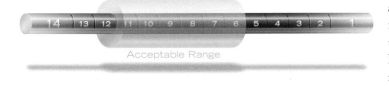

Acceptable Range

Nutrients — Macro and Micro

Other contributors to water quality are macro and micronutrients … the stuff you can't see, that makes life function. There are 17 elements that are required for life, including three macronutrients and 14 micronutrients. Macronutrients are found in commercial fertilizer mixes. When you see a fertilizer bag that says 20-10-20, these numbers refer to the percent volume of nitrogen (N), phosphorous (P), and potassium (K). These are the nutrients required in the largest quantities for proper plant growth.

Macronutrients
Nitrogen — Ammonia and nitrate are forms of nitrogen that, when in water, are usable to plants. High levels of ammonia and nitrate are very toxic to most fish. Due to this, and the fact that algae is fueled by nitrogen, it's best if these levels are undetectable or very low.

Phosphorous — In a pond situation it is best to have low or non-existent levels of phosphate. Although phosphate is not a problem for fish, it can contribute to prolific and unchecked algae growth.

Potassium - The final macronutrient is potassium. It's rare to find high levels of potassium in a pond's ecosystem. Even if you did, it wouldn't be a problem, as it is key for plant growth and fish metabolism.

Micronutrients
The other category of nutrients is micronutrients. There are 14 micronutrients required for life, and each is required in different ratios for different members of our pond-based ecosystem. They each have very specialized, important functions on the cellular level for all forms of life. These micronutrients include: boron (B), carbon (C), calcium (Ca), chlorine (Cl), copper (Cu), iron (Fe), hydrogen (H), magnesium (Mg), manganese (Mn), molybdenum (Mo), nickel (Ni), oxygen (O), phosphorous (P), sulfur (S), and zinc (Zn).

Another problem caused by excess organic matter is the depletion of oxygen. The process of leaves decomposing on the bottom of the pond can quickly consume valuable oxygen. This can be a potentially dangerous situation for the fish, especially if the pump, which provides additional oxygen, shuts off. This can be avoided by using a skimmer in the pond.

First Level of the Ecosystem

The first level of the ecosystem includes the consumers or converters. This is the biological level that makes life on earth possible. Consumers are organisms that consume waste and its chemical elements and energy from the sun, converting these into energy, mass, and life.

Tea Colored Water

One byproduct of having a small amount of organic matter decomposing at the bottom of a pond is water discoloration. This is often referred to as tea-colored water. The proper name is dissolved organic carbons, more commonly known as DOC's. These DOC's make up tannins, which are natural pigments or stains in the water.

A cup of tea has its color because of DOC's. Water that is strongly stained with DOC's tends to be slightly acidic. This stain in the water is not a bad thing in and of itself. What could be a problem, however, is a possible overload of the organic matter that causes the staining. Activated carbon, in a mesh bag in your pond, has the unique ability to pull these stains from the water.

Sixth Level
Also includes other animals
such as raccoon and deer

Fifth Level

Fourth Level

Third Le

Se

• Birds
• Snakes
• Turtles

• Fish

• Frogs • Toads
• Salamanders • Newts

• Larval Insects • Worms & Leeches
• Snails • Insects

• Zoo Plankton

• Bacteria • Phytoplankton • Protozoa • Aquatic Plants

WATER: The Base of the ECOSYSTEM

Supplemental bacteria helps keep pond water clear by consuming nutrients that would otherwise be used for algae growth.

Bacteria

Bacteria is very important in the function of an ecosystem, and there are countless types of bacteria. Bacteria prefer to be anchored in a substance like rocks or gravel, and are found in largest quantities in the midst of decomposing leaves.

Bacteria work together to form a giant recycling plant by taking waste and dead material and converting it back into usable nutrition in the food chain. An important function of bacteria is its completion of the nitrogen cycle. For starters, nitrification detoxifies fish waste (ammonia) aerobically (with oxygen). Next, anaerobic (without oxygen) bacteria denitrify nitrate into a gas that is dispersed back to the atmosphere. This is the process that we try to foster in a healthy pond ecosystem.

Phytoplankton

Phytoplankton are sun-dependent, free-floating organisms. This is a fancy way of saying free-floating algae, or "pea-soup-like" green water. There are dozens and dozens of varieties of these phytoplankton, *spirogyra, closterium,* and *anabaena* to name a few. It's never difficult finding many kinds of algae in all parts of the pond.

Helpful Tip: Putting rocks and gravel in a pond significantly reduces the amount of muck buildup in the bottom of the pond. This is because rocks and gravel provide many places for bacteria to call home, much more than with a bare liner. More bacteria means more capacity to break down fish waste and plant debris, which leads to better water quality.

Bacteria work together to form a giant recycling plant

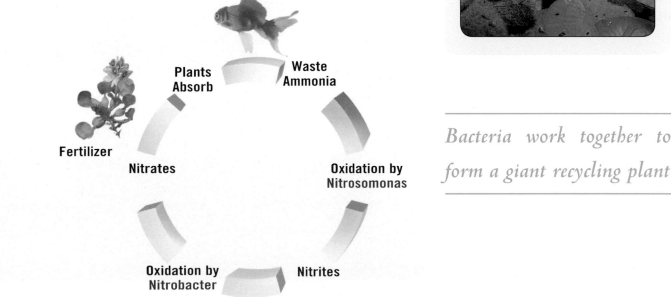

Plants Absorb → Waste Ammonia → Oxidation by Nitrosomonas → Nitrites → Oxidation by Nitrobacter → Nitrates → Fertilizer

Level
Level
Base Level

Diatoms and Protozoa

Another category of algae are diatoms. These tiny, free-floating plants tend to give the water a tan to light brown hue if they are present in large numbers (which is rare in a pond). A couple of common species of diatoms found in ponds are *asterionella* and *navicula*.

Also on this level, are protozoa. The most familiar of these tiny single-celled animals are *amoeba* and *paramecium*. They can be found free-floating in the water, and absorb nutrients, via osmosis, through their cell walls.

By far, the most visible member of the consumer-converter category are the aquatic plants.

Aquatic Plants

The final, and by far, the most visible member of the consumer-converter category are the aquatic plants. There are literally thousands of kinds from all over the world, including submerged, floating, emergent, and marginal plants. Some can be submerged 20 or more feet, while others just like their feet wet.

photo by Jacque Flannigan

The largest group of animals on earth is comprised of insects.

Second Level of the Ecosystem

The second level of the food chain is the zooplankton. These little animals are consumers. Most species of zooplankton are filter feeders. They can be found drifting through the water and sieving out food particles. They primarily eat algae, but they also consume *protozoa* and other smaller zooplankton. Some common species of zooplankton include *daphnia, cyclops,* and *rotifers.* Zooplankton are technically part of the next category (invertebrates), but because of their size, they are lower on the food chain.

Third Level of the Ecosystem

Aquatic invertebrates make up the third level of the food chain. These are part of the arthropod family, which includes all insects. It's the largest group of animals on earth. Larval insects are very common in a backyard pond. If you keep your eyes peeled, you will definitely find some type of larvae or nymph in your pond. The primary places to look would be on the bottom of the pond, in some decomposing leaves, or near the surface around the edges of the pond.

photo by Scott Hughes

Dragons in the Air

Of all the insect nymphs you may possibly find in your pond, dragonflies may be the most common, and eventually the most beautiful. Dragonflies mate in the air, and the females deposit their eggs in the pond in various places, such as on plant stems or in moist nooks along the pond's edge. The eggs hatch and the small nymphs emerge, eating just about anything including worms, other insects nymphs, or even small fish. Then, after at least three months, they will crawl out of the water onto a stem, rock, or a log, just above the water's surface, and go through the transformation into adulthood, which is called *imago*.

During their high-speed forays, a single drangonfly can consume hundreds of pesky flies, gnats, and mosquitoes each day. Their underwater nymphs offer even better pest control by consuming the developing mosquito larvae.

Larval Insects and Worms

Larval insects consume rotting organic matter, bacteria, diatoms, and zooplankton. Some of the common larval/nymph insects are: black fly larvae, caddis fly larvae, mosquito larvae, dragonfly nymph, damselfly nymph, and mayfly nymph.

Worms of many types can exist in your water garden and are harmless to you and your pets. They eat muck, detritus, and plants. The place to find these guys is right in their food, at the bottom of the pond.

Some of the common kinds of worms you may find in a pond include nematodes, tubifex worms, aquatic earthworm, horsehair worms, and planaria.

Snails

Snails primarily feed off of detritus, little dead animals, diatoms, and algae. It's common to find them under water, sucking on and scouring the rocks and gravel. They don't harm anything, though sometimes they can reproduce at prolific levels. Don't ever use chemicals to control snails. If there are too many, just do a spring clean out to decrease their food supply, and let them naturally balance themselves out. Some of the common types of snails you'll find in ponds include hairy wheel snails, little pond snails, orb snails, wrinkle snails, and the giant pond snail.

Insect Types

Water Strider

Damselflies

Dragonflies

Diving Beetle

Mayflies

Giant Water Beetle

Insects

The next, and final, category on this level of the food chain is insects in their mature form. These can primarily be found on the surface of the water and around the pond. Some of the common insects you'll see in and around your pond are water striders, whirligig beetles, water boatman, giant water bug, damselflies, dragonflies, diving beetle, mayflies, water scorpions, mosquitoes, and pill bugs. There are thousands more, but these are the most common. The majority of these insects prey on other insects, larvae, and sometimes small fish.

photo by Bill Rickert

Fourth Level of the Ecosystem

Frogs

Amphibians make up the fourth level in the pond food chain, and include hundreds of species. Frogs are probably the most renowned members of this group. They breed in the spring through early summer, which is when they constantly make their croaking sound. They lay their eggs, which then hatch into tadpoles. Frogs will eat just about anything they can get their mouths around - insects, worms, small animals, small fish, even tadpoles or other frogs. They can often be found during the day, sunning themselves on a rock or lily pad, soaking up the sun's rays. The most common types of frogs seen in ponds are leopard frogs, green frogs, bullfrogs, and pickerel frogs.

Toads

A toad might surprise you when you move a rock or skimmer lid. And no, you will not get warts from touching them. Toads have a diet similar to frogs, although they're not quite as daring when it comes to the size of their prey. You can usually find them hiding under something in a moist area. Common toads include the American toad, Fowler's toad, and the Eastern spadefoot toad.

Salamanders and Newts

Salamanders and newts are very hard to find in backyard ponds. Even in regions where they exist, only about one in 10 ponds will have them. If you have them in your pond, you should feel lucky. They feed on worms, insects, and larvae, and can be found in moist spots full of organic matter. If you're lucky, you can see them in their juvenile form in the pond. The most common newts and salamanders you may see in your pond are the red spotted newt, spotted salamander, tiger salamander, mud salamander, red-backed salamanders, two-lined salamanders, and the dusky salamander.

Red Spotted Newt

Spotted Salamander

Fifth Level of the Ecosystem

Fish

On the fifth level of the pond food chain we find fish. In a natural pond, you may find bass, bluegill, sunfish, the common carp, or any number of other kinds of fish. In the backyard pond, the most common fish include koi, goldfish, and shubunkins. Each have its own diet preferences, but most are omnivorous, meaning they'll eat just about anything. They eat worms, nymphs, larvae, other fish, algae, detritus and tadpoles. For more detailed information on fish, see Chapter 6.

Sixth Level of the Ecosystem

This sixth level of the food chain is the connection to the surrounding environment. This is where the backyard pond begins to contribute to the big picture, the regional environment.

Birds

The main top-end predator of the pond and its inhabitants are birds. Their diet consists of various aquatic life. Most birds love fish, aquatic plants, crustaceans, and any other tasty morsels they can fit between their beaks.

The primary hunter in most ponds is the great blue heron. These birds love ornamental pond fish because they're easy targets to catch. Although rare, other birds that prey upon pond inhabitants include hawks, osprey, egret, green heron, kingfisher, and an occasional eagle. For the most part, geese, swan, and all types of ducks prefer a diet of aquatic vegetation but will consume some smaller pond animals.

A bird of prey is usually an unwanted visitor to the backyard pond because of the expensive ornamental fish they may eat. If you can, try to co-exist with them as much as possible. If you need help controlling these guests, see the section in Chapter 6 under 'predator control.'

photos.com

Great Blue Heron

Green Heron

Egret

Reptiles

Reptiles, snakes, and turtles are very misunderstood, and therefore, most people fear them. These animals eat almost anything in the pond ecosystem, but nothing in the pond eats them.

Snakes

Snakes eat fish and frogs rather frequently. The good thing about snakes is that they also eat pesky rodents commonly found around the yard. Most ponds will not have snakes, but if you find one, don't be alarmed. Just be cautious when you open the skimmer box or tinker around the pond so you don't provoke them. Some of the common kinds of snakes you'll find around ponds are garter snakes, blacksnakes, and common water snakes.

Garter Snake

The good thing about snakes is that they also eat pesky rodents commonly found around the yard.

Turtle Types

Painted Turtle

Mud Turtle

Pond Slider

Turtles make very tame and wonderful pets.

Turtles

Turtles are a more welcome addition to a pond. Large turtles can eat fish, and they do so in natural lakes and ponds. Typically, in backyard ponds, turtles don't eat fish. Instead, they prefer to munch on fish food and all sorts of vegetation. They actually make very tame and wonderful pets. Some common turtles are musk turtles, mud turtles, painted turtles, pond sliders, and spiny softshell turtles.

Other Animals

Other animals that spend time near the pond and depend on the pond ecosystem for some part of their food or water source include raccoons and deer. Naturally, animals are dependent on water, so a pond is very inviting to them.

A pond shortly after construction.

The same pond after adding landscape decoration.

How Does Pond Building Affect the Ecosystem?

As we understand how ponds work and what plants and animals live in them, we learn to appreciate nature instead of being afraid of it.

Do you want your pond to be more diverse? Given time and some proper plant selection in and around the pond, you can create a very diverse ecosystem in your yard. Just remember to keep it simple, and with patience your pond will mature over the years into a beautiful part of nature.

One pond in one backyard may not seem very important, but when you have a thousand similar backyard ecosystems functioning simultaneously, there's truly a positive impact being made on the environment. Large amounts of habitat are restored for frogs, toads, newts, and salamanders. The population of each of these creatures have been declining sharply for many years now. Birds have also been driven from many of their natural wetland habitats, which they need so desperately to survive. Your pond will provide a safe haven for these creatures and add a welcome diversity to our stressed suburban environments.

Chapter 11

Building Your Pond

Putting it All Together

Synergy is when all parts of the puzzle work together so effectively that the whole is greater than the sum of the parts. It's that intangible piece of magic that distinguishes great athletic teams apart from the not-so-great. It's what makes a great piece of art or music immediately stand out from all the rest. It's no different for a naturally-beautiful, balanced, aquatic ecosystem. Done right, the whole is greater than the sum of its parts.

When shopping for the parts that will make up your water garden, it's important to make sure that they work together to create a low-maintenance water gardening experience. Buying your pond parts in the form of a kit is the best way to achieve this, but it's still in your best interest to understand the function of each one.

Choosing the Liner

A solid foundation for a house is extremely important. You would not build your home's foundation out of sand just because it is the least expensive material available. The same logic holds true when choosing a liner for a pond.

The liner is the pond's foundation. Choosing an inferior liner can lead to a leaky pond and many possible headaches. Start with a good foundation and you will be able to sleep at night knowing your pond will hold water for years to come. The first step in choosing the proper liner is to educate yourself on the selection of liners that are available and decide which is best for your application.

Warranty

Don't even consider using a liner if it doesn't come with a long-term warranty. Many liners come with a 20-year warranty which state that the liner will not prematurely deteriorate because of weathering within a 20-year period. The sun's ultraviolet rays are the primary culprit in the deterioration of most liners. The liner in a pond built with boulders and gravel covering the liner will be protected from ultraviolet rays, further extending its lifespan well beyond 20 years.

What Is Fish Safe?

It is important to also determine whether the liner you choose is safe for fish, or any other critters, that may inhabit your water garden. A liner that is fish safe is guaranteed by the manufacturer to be chemically compounded so it is safe for fish. Each fish safe liner is tested, and should come with a stamp indicating that it is safe.

Many people use liner that is not stamped as fish safe without a problem. There also have been reports of pond owners with dead fish in their new ponds, built without fish safe liner. The reason? Liner manufacturers use a wide variety of raw materials to produce their liners, and quite often the cost of one raw material might increase, causing the manufacturer to choose a less expensive substitute raw material. Some of these substitutes may not be safe for aquatic life. This would help explain why people sometimes get away without using fish safe liner, while others have dead fish. If you plan on putting fish in your water garden, it's just not worth the risk!

Start with a good foundation and you will be able to sleep at night knowing your pond will hold water for years to come.

Which Type of Liner?

45 mil EPDM Rubber
This material is durable, puncture resistant, and flexible. Flexibility comes in very handy when working with the irregular twists, turns, and shelves commonly found in a pond or stream. Durability helps in preventing leaks from puncturing, especially when it comes to placing large boulders on the liner.

40 mil Polypropylene
Durable, 40 mil polypropylene is actually more durable and puncture resistant than 45 mil EPDM. However, it's limited flexibility makes it difficult to work with, especially when using it in very small water gardens with tight spaces.

Polypropylene is a few cents per square foot more expensive than EPDM. This can add up quickly on a large project. In larger ponds, its performance and durability can be well worth the extra dollars.

30 mil Polyethylene
For large water garden projects with tight budget constraints, 30 mil polyethylene is a consideration. Unfortunately, the only real advantage of polyethylene is its cost. It's about half the price of polypropylene and EPDM. It can also be difficult to work with. Cheaper isn't always better, and in this case, you get what you pay for. Polyethylene is not nearly as flexible as EPDM or polypropylene either. It is a plastic-type liner and can be stiff to work with.

Underlayment
The underlayment is installed before the liner in order to prevent any punctures that may occur from rough or rocky ground. Many different types of materials have been used for this in the past. The best material is the one that is easy to use, cost effective, and readily available. Favored for its convenience, is a non-woven geotextile fabric. It's lightweight, effective, and easy to use.

This underlayment actually serves a couple of purposes. It not only provides protection for the liner against rocky

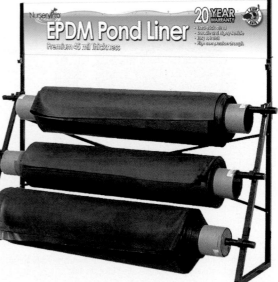

> *The liner is one of the largest investments in your pond project and the most difficult to replace.*

soils and roots, but it also allows the ground to breathe from underneath. You see, the earth releases gases all the time, and the fabric allows the gases to escape from underneath the liner rather than becoming trapped and causing gas bubbles to push the liner up into the pond.

There are disadvantages to using materials like old carpet remants and newspaper as an underlayment. Although the material is inexpensive, if not free, it can be difficult to work with. Have you ever tried to paper mache´ the bottom of a pond … on a windy day?

Carpet remnants can be very heavy, difficult to work with, and are often difficult to come by. Another common liner padding is sand. Yes, sand will be effective for the horizontal surfaces in your pond, but that's it. There is no way for sand to protect the vertical edges inside the pond, where roots may penetrate or a sharp rock or object is imbedded in the side of the shelf.

Favored for its convenience, This underlayment is a non-woven, geotextile fabric. It's lightweight, effective, and easy to use.

Plumbing, Pumps, and Electrical

Plumbing … A Key Component of Pond Building
A well-designed water feature includes many components and construction materials for installation. One key component is a re-circulation system, which requires plumbing.

There are several different methods used in plumbing these days. There are different kinds of pipe, many random components, and a wide array of fittings. Knowing and choosing what to use can be confusing and overwhelming.

Schedule 40 PVC
The cheap cost of this material makes it the most commonly used plumbing material in the country. It is strong and rigid but, because it is only sold in ten-foot increments, it can be

Flexible PVC piping dramatically simplifies assembly and increases productivity.

difficult to transport. The need for 45° and 90° elbows to make turns in the piping can take extra time to glue the fittings. These turns may also most likely restrict the water flow. PVC pipe is susceptible to cracking during the freeze/thaw cycle of most zones.

Poly Pipe

Poly pipe was originally designed for use in the irrigation industry. It's large size can make this material difficult to work with. A 100' roll of 2" poly pipe stands over 5 1/2' feet tall and can be extremely hard to work with once unpackaged. Another disadvantage is the fact that a rubber mallet, barbed fittings, and metal clamps are necessary for making connections. Together, these points indicate that this material is inconvenient and extremely labor intensive to use.

Flexible PVC

This product came from the pool and spa industry. It can handle sharp turns and tight corners, eliminating the need for tees and elbows. Since it expands and contracts with seasonal changes, it is not necessary to drain for the winter, making it easy and low maintenance in cold climates.

Fittings

There are enough fittings to fill the pages of an entire book. The need for various fittings and their uses depends upon the type of pipe and

filtration system that you use to build your pond.

Choosing a Pump — Establishing The Flow Rate

The first, and most important step, before you even begin to look for a pump, is to establish a desired flow rate for the waterfall and stream.

For each foot of waterfall width, you need 1,500 gallons per hour (gph) of water flow from your pump. This is a good "rule of thumb" that will help ensure that you have enough water to cover the entire width of the waterfall and stream that you build.

Example #1: If you're building a waterfall that is two feet wide, you want a pump that will produce approximately 3,000 gph.

Example #2: If you 're building a waterfall that is 10 feet wide, you'll need a pump(s) that would produce a total of 15,000 gph.

Typical Parts of a Pump

Note: Check Valve attaches to pipe leading out from discharge

Discharge

Motor

Impeller Housing

Intake

Feet Motor Housing Impeller

This "rule of thumb" does not mean that the entire stream has to be the same width. Be creative by narrowing down the stream in spots to create racing rapids, or expand the stream slightly to create a babbling brook. This provides an attractive amount of water. Not so much that it's overpowering, and not so little that it looks like a leaky faucet.

How Much Water Does the Pump Really Pump?

Many people assume that a pump rated at 3,000 gph will always push 3,000 gph. This is far from true. In reality, this will only happen under a light workload. The pump, as soon as you subject it to a higher waterfall height or a longer pipe run, will push less and less water until it reaches its "shut-off height."

The shut-off height, which is different for every pump, is the point at which the pump is exposed to so much of a workload that it can no longer push any water. Avoid the "leaky faucet" dilemma by using the shut-off height as a guideline. If the height of your waterfall comes near the listed shut-off height, you can eliminate that pump from your selection.

photo by Mark Pastor

Chapter 12

Pond Construction

Getting Off to the Right Start

It may seem really basic, but it's extremely important to know how to properly excavate or dig a pond. Anyone can dig a hole, but do you really know the benefits of doing it right? A step-by-step process will undoubtedly save you time, money, materials, and headaches. To get off on the right foot and avoid surprises later on, there are a couple of things to do before the digging starts.

Assess the property where the pond will be located and take note of any existing structures and utilities. Using a level, determine and adjust the high and low areas where the pond will be positioned.

On the Level

As you dig your pond, it is important to make sure that all of the edges are level. This is not only to avoid an unexpected low edge, which can later cause a leak, but also to make sure that the skimmer sits at the proper height to skim. There are several different methods that can be used to level a pond, depending on the resources that are available.

The most accurate method is to use a builder or sight level, taking several readings around the perimeter of the pond. Since this type of level will likely need to be rented or bought, it may not be the most practical option for a one-time installation. There are two other options that make use of more common household tools and may be more convenient. First, you can take a standard 2"x 4" board and lay it across the pond with a common bubble level resting on the center. The level will show if the two sides are even, and all sides can be measured in the same way by changing the direction of the board across the pond.

The second method is to use a line level. A line level is basically a small bubble level attached to the end of a string. The other end of the string is then attached to a stake that is placed at any point around the perimeter of the pond. The level is then walked around the pond and readings are taken at several different points to ensure the sides are even. Remember, the pond does not have to be perfectly level, but general readings should be taken to avoid any major problems.

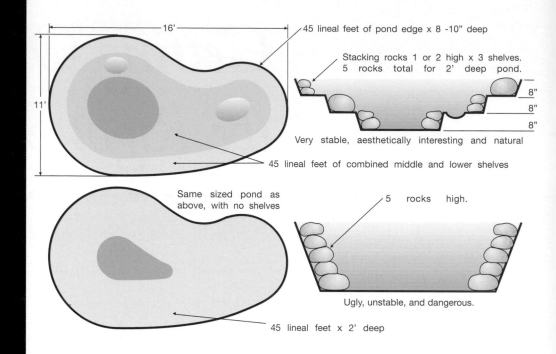

45 lineal feet of pond edge x 8 -10" deep

Stacking rocks 1 or 2 high x 3 shelves. 5 rocks total for 2' deep pond.

8"
8"
8"

Very stable, aesthetically interesting and natural

45 lineal feet of combined middle and lower shelves

Same sized pond as above, with no shelves

5 rocks high.

Ugly, unstable, and dangerous.

45 lineal feet x 2' deep

Digging the Pond

It may seem really basic, but it's extremely important to know how to properly excavate, or dig your pond. Anyone can dig a hole, but there are benefits in doing it right.

You'll first need to assess the property where the pond will be located. Look for a level area for the pond, ideally with an adjacent slope that faces your viewing area. The slope will be used to build the waterfall later on. Mark the area by outlining it with spray paint or a garden hose. This will help you visualize what the shape will look like next to any surrounding landscape features.

The Site Assessment

Go around the ponds perimeter to determine the high and low areas in relation to the main viewing area. Most water gardens are located next to a patio, so the patio would be the starting point. Most people like the water to come right up to the viewing area – often a patio – so the water level should be set 2-3" below the level of the patio Once the water level is established, make sure the entire pond perimeter is a minimum of 2" above the established water level. *All measurements taken from this point forward will be in direct relationship to the water level!*

At the back edge of the pond, where the waterfall is located, the level would be much higher, depending on the final waterfall height.

Don't Forget the Shelves

There are a number of important benefits in a pond built with shelves.

Safety – If someone were to accidentally, or purposefully, walk into the pond, it would be like walking down a gradual staircase, not a steep and slippery, dangerous drop-off or slope.

Strength and Stability – Terracing is much more stable and less likely to collapse than a steep, tall wall.

Aesthetics – If the water garden is built and filtered properly, the water will be very clear, and you will see the bottom of the pond. The contours of the shelves add interest to the pond's interior.

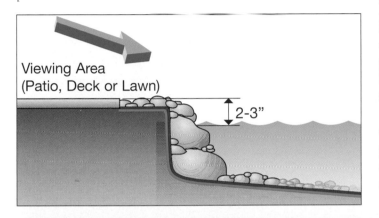

Aquatic plants – Ledges in a pond provide the ideal water depths for the many different aquatic plant species that are available for naturalized pondscaping.

Marginals require a water depth of 1-12" depending on the plant type. Water lilies prefer 12-36" of water. If they are planted in water less than 12" deep, they may not overwinter. Oxygenators prefer 12-36" of water depth.

The First Ledge

Now you're ready to dig the first ledge. It's typically 6-10" deep and should be dug around the perimeter of the entire pond. Remember, this ledge will be covered in gravel, so a ledge that is 6" deep will become 4" deep after the gravel is installed.

Ledges can vary according to their usage, but they *do not* have to be perfect. Remember, the goal is to copy nature, and natural ponds don't have perfectly level or symmetrical ledges graduating toward the bottom of the pond. When the first ledge is completed, mark out the next area to be excavated.

The deeper you can dig, the better the better the pond will look.

Helpful Tip:
Shelves that are too big in proportion to the size of the pond will create problems when placing boulders along the edge of the vertical walls. The pond will literally look like a pit of rocks rather than a water garden.

The size of the berm should be in proportion to the size of the pond and the height of the waterfall.

Berm Building

Don't haul away any of the soil that you remove as you're digging your pond. This can be used to build a berm around your waterfall. The size of the berm should be in proportion to the size of the pond and the height of the waterfall. In other words, if the pond is 11' x 16', and 2' deep, the berm should be 11' x 16' and 2' feet high. Each site is different and should be evaluated based on the natural topography of the area.

Soil usage is often an overlooked part of the construction process. Soil is rarely removed, however, if the quality of the soil from the excavation is poor, organic topsoil should be brought in and used to top the berm for the benefit of the plants that you add later.

Challenges of Poor Soil Conditions

There are many soil types that can cause all sorts of construction challenges, for example:

Clay Soil – Spring and fall are the best times for excavation because the clay is softer, while mid-summer could require a pick-ax to chisel through the hardened clay.

Rocky Soil – In addition to longer digging time, rocky soil can be damaging to your liner. After the digging is complete, lay down several layers of underlayment to act as additional cushion under the liner. In severe cases, place a layer of the fabric on top of the liner where larger boulders will be set.

Bedrock – Bedrock is tougher because it takes much longer to dig than any other soil type. Depending on where the

Use soil excavated from the pond area to build up the berm around the BIOFALLS® filter. This illustration is intended to show the location for the removed soil. The shape of the berm should be adapted to whatever shape you desire. Just make sure to completely surround the BIOFALLS® filter with soil, and make the berm descend gradually to the water's edge to prevent erosion into the pond.

rock layer is found, the pond may need to be built partially above grade. The deeper down you can dig, the better the pond will look. It can be tough to make a pond look natural when it's sitting 18" above the surrounding soil.

Sandy Soil – In sandy, loose soils the digging is a piece of cake, but it's almost impossible to cut a ledge into it. The easiest way to handle this problem is to dig the pond with a flat bottom, with the side gently sloping into the middle. Once the pond is dug, you have two options. One is to place boulders on the sloping sides, and put gravel on the bottom. The other option is to place boulders on the bottom and backfill behind the rocks, creating gravel and boulder terraces. Planting areas and irregular ledges can be created with this method.

Helpful Tip:
Tools to build your backyard pond are readily available. They include:
Sturdy shovel – Rough excavation.
Flat shovel – Finishing and shaping.
Pick-axe – Tough soil.
Pry bar – Removing larger stones.
Wheelbarrow – Moving materials.
Site level – Accuracy of project.

The only specialized item that's required is a site level. Most individuals don't own one, and no one really wants to purchase one at $250 to $300 a throw. They can, however, be rented for about $30 a day at a rental yard.

Waterfalls and Streams

What's the Attraction?

Waterfalls and streams capture the imagination of all who witness their beauty. Many people go on long, exhausting treks into the wilderness just to see a section of a river, a waterfall, or a stream. They're beautiful and inspiring, but why do we seek them out? Maybe it's the feeling of being one with nature or the contemplative feeling of peace we find within ourselves.

The bottom line is, waterfalls and streams are an amazing part of the world we live in. They deliver and clean the water that's so vital to our existence.

Starting With the Basics

The pond is built, and you're now ready to start working on the stream and waterfall. You have all the components, you know the rock that you're using, the style of falls, and you know where the stream is starting and ending. So, how do you connect them in an interesting, yet functional manner? The easiest way is to follow Mother Nature's designs.

A man-made waterfall is simply water pumped from one body of water to an area above that body of water. Then it wells up and falls back down with the help of gravity. If you do it right, it'll look good, sound good, and not lose any water in between.

You need to think about the effect you'd like to achieve. Do you want a peaceful trickle or thundering rapids? Are you trying to drown out traffic noise from a nearby road or are you looking to mimic the sounds of nature?

Waterfalls and streams deliver and clean the water that's so vital to our existence.

These decisions will help determine the type of rock that you choose and the size pump that you need for your pond.

The Stream and Its Waterfalls

As you design, layout, and create the stream portion of your water garden, there are a few tips to keep in mind as you create the most naturalistic stream possible.

Remember, water wants to run downhill as quickly as possible, and along the way it hits objects that are harder than the surrounding soil (large rocks and logs), and encounters sharp elevation changes. When this happens, the water moves off course, and the new watercourse continues downhill until it hits another object, and the cycle starts all over again. The larger the hill, the greater

---

The easiest way to create a waterfall is to follow Mother Nature's designs.

---

the odds of the water hitting objects. The goal is to copy this look as much as possible.

Your stream should twist and turn as it makes its way toward the pond. The turns will increase the sounds, and will also increase the number of viewing areas. The more places it can be seen, the more it'll be enjoyed.

A large rock should be placed at each turn. It doesn't have to be huge, but it should be larger than the aver-

A beautiful, meandering stream and waterfall in an area that before, was a plain grass backyard.

Pond builders salivate when they have slopes to work with ... you have a better template to work with. After a while, every slope you pass without a waterfall will look incomplete.

In nature, water carves the earth out of many thousands of years to form a waterfall. We only have a couple of hours.

Every stone has a place.

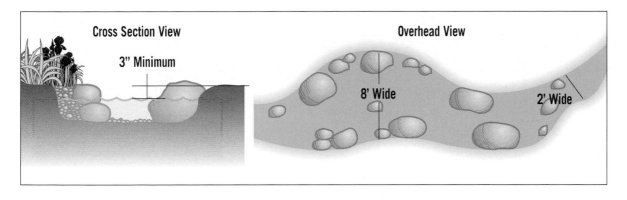

Cross Section View

3" Minimum

Overhead View

8' Wide

2' Wide

age rocks in your pond. At elevation changes, place additional larger stones, or a series of stones, to replicate the erosion process.

Getting Creative With the Stream

The stream should get narrow in areas, and then widen out and slow down in others. Make sure you use a good mix of stone and gravel to create a natural look.

Adding moss to a job is the finishing touch. It is often the only green amongst a sea of mulch and rocks.

Helpful Tip:

There are many factors that determine how water will act in a given situation and because of this, there is no standard formula. The results vary according to the pitch of the streambed, the width, rock positions, rock size, water flow, shape of the stream, and how the water exits the stream.

Although there are no concrete rules, following a simple set of guidelines will help create a natural looking stream.

- Always slope the streambed toward the pond.
- Have areas within the stream where the water can pool.
- If the stream narrows in one place, open it back up downstream.
- Leave several inches of soil and liner above the proposed water level in the stream.
- High water flow rates need a wider stream and/or higher edges.

Two Grande BIOFALLS® filters with two pumps created this double waterfall.

A waterfall should look good with or without water.

Fill the streambed with aquatic plants, and you've just created an awesome supplement to your filtration system.

The hardest part about streams is learning how the water reacts in certain situations. When a stream is long and without much slope, the water will tend to move too slowly, causing water to well up along the sides. This can become a problem if the edges aren't high enough.

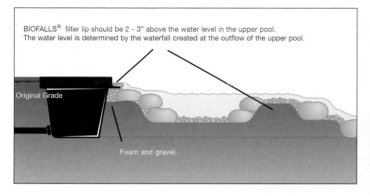

BIOFALLS® filter lip should be 2 - 3" above the water level in the upper pool. The water level is determined by the waterfall created at the outflow of the upper pool.

Original Grade

Foam and gravel,

photo by Scott Hughes

Building a Beautiful Waterfall

There are many ways to build a waterfall for your pond. Often the result is a waterfall that leaks or looks like a chimney stack spewing water. The easiest way to build waterfall is to use a biological filter. Easy to hide, they give you a good base for building a leak-free, beautiful waterfall with the benefit of additional filtration. Biological filters are extremely flexible, and a variety of different waterfall styles can be created even when there isn't a lot of space.

One More Thing Before You Get Started

You may be anxious to get out and start building a dreamscape with lots of flowing water and a serene pond filled with lilies and extraordinary koi. Before you get your marking paint and shovel out, there's one more greatly misunderstood concept of pond and stream construction to talk about here.

It seems that many people are so enthralled with the sound of water, that all they want is a huge waterfall and stream that fills their property with the incredible sounds of falling water. The only problem is, if the pond gets neglected, and/or forgotten about, it doesn't work very well. So, let your creativity take over and use the tips to create an aquatic paradise in your own backyard, keeping everything in proportion. Mother Nature will appreciate it, and so will you … in the long run. 🍃

Chapter 13

The ABC's of Pond Care

Your Glossary to Maintenance and Troubleshooting

Algae

ALGAE is a natural part of any healthy ecosystem. Simply an aquatic weed, algae will thrive on any excess nutrients found in a pond's water chemistry. Excess nutrients can come from a variety of sources (like decomposed organic debris, fish waste, fish food and fertilizers). Often, the difficult part of algae control is narrowing down the main source of the problem and taking the appropriate counter-measures. Remember, when dealing with Mother Nature, algae control preventions and remedies will limit the growth of algae, but it will never make a pond completely algae-free. Only chemically-treated water features can maintain a truly algae-free status. Unfortunately, these systems are unable to support fish and plant life, and take away from the overall lifestyle of water gardening.

The following list contains the five key ingredients to developing a natural ecosystem in your water garden. Failure to duplicate these five elements will only increase the potential for excessive algae growth.

1. A **Circulation System** is really just a fancy way of saying "pumps and plumbing." The proper size pump and pipe diameter are extremely important for the aesthetics of a water feature. More importantly, an efficient circulation system

Aquatic Plants

Fish

Filtration System

Circulation System

Rocks, Gravel and Bacteria

There are five key ingredients to developing a natural ecosystem in your water garden.

keeps the water moving and provides the necessary oxygen levels for healthy fish and plants.

2. A **Proper Filtration System** includes the use of both a biological and a mechanical filter. A biological filter provides surface area for beneficial bacteria to colonize and remove excess nutrients from the water. A mechanical filter will not only pre-filter the water and house the pump, it will also skim debris from the water's surface to

prevent the accumulation of organic materials on the pond floor.

3. **Fish** are an integral part of any ecosystem. Unfortunately, fish are often seen as creating a maintenance nightmare. Contrary to popular belief, fish will actually reduce pond maintenance, as they graze on string algae and bottom feed from the pond floor.

4. **Aquatic Plants** are Mother Nature's true filters. Plants are great for adding character to a pond by providing color and texture, but from a filtration perspective, they're second to none. Thriving from the excess nutrients in a pond and depriving algae of its food source, the aquatic plants in

a water garden, given proper coverage, are critical for the overall health of the ecosystem.

5. **Rocks, Gravel, and Bacteria** have been a controversial element in the industry for many years. Many enthusiasts have steered away from rocks and gravel out of fear that their system will become a maintenance nightmare. On the contrary, rocks and gravel will not only protect pond liners from UV light degradation, but they will also provide tremendous surface area for beneficial bacteria to break down excess nutrients in the water and dissolved organic debris on the pond floor.

photo by Scott Hughes

Feeding fish a handful of high-protein food once a day is plenty.

There are hundreds of different types of algae with all sorts of scientific names, but they can basically be broken down into two categories: green water and string algae. Following these simple prevention steps and remedies will limit the excessive growth of either.

Prevention

Cleaning the Biological Filter on a regular basis is counterproductive and shouldn't be done more than once a year. Cleaning the filter regularly will simply destroy the colonies of beneficial bacteria that clean the pond water.

Controlling Leaks will limit the amount of fresh, nutrient-rich, water that is added to replenish a leaky pond. The nutrient-rich water will only contribute to future algae blooms and disrupt the balance of the ecosystem.

Controlling Run-Off into a pond is extremely important. Ponds in low "retention" areas are far more susceptible to this problem and will most likely suffer the consequences. Run-off water contains many harmful elements, such as ground fertilizers and other various chemicals found on city streets. These elements are not desired in ponds, and should be avoided.

Overfeeding the Fish is a common mistake made by well-intended enthusiasts. Understand that an outdoor water feature is much different from an indoor aquarium. Outdoors, the natural ecosystem will provide for fish, so feeding fish a handful

of high-protein food once a day is plenty. If excessive algae blooms completely overrun the pond, fish feeding should be stopped altogether, as it will only contribute to the algae problem.

Overstocking the Pond with fish is also a common mistake that leads to poor water quality conditions. Overstocking will not only raise the ammonia to unhealthy levels and stress the fish, but it will also add to undesired, high nutrient levels, because of the overwhelming amount of fish waste. Again, the high nutrient levels will simply act as a food source for new algae blooms.

Removing Debris from a water feature is usually taken care of by a mechanical skimmer filter, but not all systems have such a device. Organic debris that falls to the water's surface will eventually become waterlogged and sink to the pond floor. It's only a matter of time before that debris begins to break down and decompose. The decomposition of such materials can release toxic elements into the water and raise nutrient levels.

-

Remedies

Barley straw or barley extract has been used successfully in water treatment for many years. Barley will not destroy existing algae in a pond, but it will stunt the algae's growth and prevent future growth. The barley begins to decompose in six to eight weeks, leaving natural

peroxides that have been scientifically proven to break down the cell walls of algae, reducing the capability of new cell growth.

Flocculants are commonly used in ponds with green water problems. This type of remedy works by coagulating suspended particulates of organic material through a process known as flocculation. This allows all suspended organics, including suspended algae, to be attracted together and easily removed.

Koi, simply ornamental carp, are bottom feeders by nature. Larger koi will clean the pond by scavenging off the pond floor and grazing on most string algae in the pond.

Natural Bacteria and Enzymes will attach themselves to any available surface area found inside a pond and its filtration system. Once seeded, bacteria will grow by consuming available nutrients and utilizing oxygen found in the system.

Alternative Remedies

Certain sodium-based algae control remedies, which also contain natural bacteria and

> *Like fine wine, ponds mature with age, so don't be surprised or concerned if a new pond has instant algae problems.*

enzymes, are available to hinder algae's ability to absorb calcium in the water. Since algae is dependent on calcium to create its structure, the lack of it will cause the weed to become brittle, crack, and break away from the surface upon which it grew. Just be careful not to over-treat the pond. Too much of this remedy can affect the other plants in the pond.

Illustration by Tony Mancha

UV Lights are filter accessories that, when used correctly, will effectively control the suspended algae (green water) in a pond. Unlike a natural reme-dy, an ultraviolet clari-fier will damage algae

cells by attacking them with ultraviolet radiation. However, this synthetic remedy will have very little effect on string algae.

Be Patient!

Creating a balanced ecosystem doesn't just happen overnight! Like fine wine, ponds mature with age, so don't be sur-prised or concerned if a new pond has instant algae problems. Once the plants, fish, and bacteria are established, the algae will decrease, as will the amount of maintenance on the pond, however, most ponds will undergo an algae cycle every year. In colder climates, the plants, fish, and bacteria will go dormant dur-ing the winter, creating advantageous conditions for algae growth. Without competition, the algae will take full advantage of the available nutrients in the pond. Do not be discouraged if the pond resembles pea soup or is full of string algae during this time of the year. When the warmer temperatures return and stabilize, the ecosystem will regenerate itself, and the algae growth will once again decrease. Understand that environmental conditions play a huge role in water quality, and that some ponds will take longer than others to achieve a proper balance.

*A*quatic Plants

AQUATIC PLANTS can make or break a water garden. Thousands of varieties of plants are available in all sorts of col-ors and textures, and they will definitely expand the overall enjoyment of a water garden. The best thing about plants is how

easy they are to maintain. A pond without plants would be like a yard with no trees or bushes. Besides the aesthetic value that plants bring, they are also one of the essen-tial components in developing a healthy ecosystem. They are Mother Nature's fil-ters and will help keep a pond clean.

Starting Out

You don't have to be a landscape archi-tect to figure out that tall, ornamental

Note: Certain aquatic plants, like lotus, are extremely invasive and, if allowed, will completely take over. Plants like these should be left in their pots.

grasses should not be planted in front of the main viewing area. The point is to keep the pond's viewing areas in mind when selecting and planting aquatic plants. Also, keep in mind sunlight conditions that could affect a plant's ability to grow. Finally, lose the pots! A plant that sits in a pot too long will only become "root-bound" and won't grow to its full potential. Because there is no planting media available in a bare liner pond, potted plants must be used and will need to be divided and repotted every few years. Ponds that utilize the benefits of a gravel substrate have the perfect environment for bareroot aquatic plants to thrive. Simply clear an area of gravel, place the aquatic plant and its soil directly on the pond liner, and backfill the area with the same gravel.

Throughout the season

As for the plants throughout the season, you can just leave them alone. They'll be fine. On occasion, certain aquatic plants could use a little extra something to help them reach their

Warning: Aquatic plant fertilizers should not be used if the pond is suffering from poor water quality.

blooming potential. Aquatic fertilizer tablets are available for just that purpose.

Winterization

Cutting plants back before winter is always a good idea. If a plant's dead foliage is allowed to decompose in the water over the winter, the pond's water quality will suffer. Climate will determine if tropical plants can be left in the pond over the winter, or if they can simply be treated as annuals and replaced each season.

Spring Maintenance

Dividing aquatic plants in the spring will keep a water garden looking sharp. However, this type of maintenance may not be necessary every year. Aesthetics are usually the determining factor as to whether a pond owner divides the plants in a pond. If the pond's water surface is no longer visible, then it's probably about time to divide. Share your plants with a neighbor, or dump the waste in a compost pile.

Biological Filter
See Filters

Clean-out
See Spring Clean-outs

Debris
See Water Quality

Cutting back plant material in the fall will prevent organic debris from decomposing in the water over the winter.

The BIOFALLS® filter creates the perfect base for creating beautiful waterfalls.

Electrical – See Pumps/Plumbing

Filters

Filters are the synthetic elements that help keep our ponds clean. Without filtration systems incorporated into man-made water features, good water quality would be much more difficult to maintain. There are many different filters made for the water garden industry. There isn't necessarily a right or wrong type of filter, as long as there is an understanding of how various filters work and how they should be maintained.

A **Biological Waterfall Filter** works by utilizing the power of natural bacteria and enzymes to consume excess nutrients and break down organic materials found in the water. This type of filter relies on available surface area for beneficial bacteria to seed and grow, therefore, filtration media inside these filters must be available. Over time, sludge and other solid waste will accumulate in the filter media and must be cleaned in order to sustain bacterial life. Just remember to only clean the filtration media when the spring clean-out is performed. Washing down the media and depriving the bacteria of necessary oxygen is counterproductive when maintaining a balanced ecosystem.

The **Mechanical Skimmer Filter** was developed to help trap sediment and particles in pond water. Trapping the suspended materials will help keep the water clear and act as a pre-filter for the pump. By skimming the water's surface of floating debris, a mechanical filter helps reduce the amount of material that becomes water-logged and sinks to the pond floor. Organic material allowed to decompose in the pond will only result in poor water quality. Regular maintenance on a filter of this type requires you to remove the large debris that the filter catches and to periodically clean the filter media to prevent clogging. If the filter media does become clogged, a dramatic loss in flow rate of the waterfall pump may be noticed.

A **Pressurized Filter** basically serves the same purpose as any other pond filter out there; it cleans water. This particular type of canister or container filter is powered and pressurized by a water pump and is often located outside of the pond. There is only one point of entry in a filter of this nature, which increases

Cleaning the biological filter shouldn't be done more than once a year.

pressure and forces water through the unit. The water must pass through several layers of biological media and an optional ultraviolet clarifier before it is forced through its one exit point and eventually back into the pond. Maintenance on a pressurized filter is very similar to that of every other filter. Cleaning the media inside the unit is absolutely necessary for the filter to operate properly.

Certain filters have a bypass outlet, which will allow the water to continue flowing even when the filter media is clogged. Some filters even have LED indicator lights that signal when the system needs to be cleaned. The only other regular maintenance necessary on units that include the optional ultraviolet clarifier is replacement of the UV light bulbs. These are effective at removing all single-celled particles and other suspended material in water, including parasites and harmful bacteria, but the individual light bulbs won't last forever. Again, some pressure filters may have an LED indicator light that also signals when the UV light is down.

A well-balanced ecosystem will contain all of the essential elements needed to support fish life.

Fish

Fish maintenance is generally a very basic task. The bottom line in proper fish care comes down to maintaining healthy environmental conditions in the pond. A well-balanced ecosystem will contain all of the essential elements needed to support fish life. Unfortunately, outdoor systems are susceptible to many harmful elements that exist in nature, and sometimes these unwanted elements make their way into our ponds. Certain bacterial infections and diseases may result in fish death, and many times, this is out of our control. Identifying behavioral disorders and physical symptoms early is key to saving our finned friends.

Many fish-care products are available to treat and maintain fish health. Besides providing a healthy environment, there is not much to fish keeping. For the health of the fish, a good rule of thumb is to not exceed one inch of fish length per square foot of the pond. See **Winterization** for proper fish care over the winter.

A good rule of thumb is to not exceed an inch of fish per square foot of the pond.

Ground Settling – See Leaks

Heron – See dictionary definition for **Nuisance**

Ice

It's okay and safe for your fish if your pond is covered in ice, as long as a hole is left in it so gases can escape and oxygen is circulating. See **Winterization.**

Jealousy

Unfortunately, there is no cure for your neighbors envy of your pond. Sorry.

Koi

Koi is a popular ornamental fish related to the carp. See **Fish** for care.

Leaks

Leaks are going to happen. The good thing is that most leaks are extremely easy to solve. The first step is to determine if the pond actually has a leak, or if innocent evaporation is the culprit. Unfortunately, there are hundreds of factors that will determine a pond's true evaporation rate (i.e. surface area of a pond, climate, full sun, half sun, no sun, multiple waterfalls, height of waterfalls, amount of splash, stream length, pump size, etc.). On average, ponds will lose anywhere from one to two inches of water in a week, through evaporation. However, ponds in warmer climates could potentially lose one to two inches in a single day during the heat of summer.

Once evaporation is ruled out, a determination needs to be made as to whether or not the pond itself is holding water. To determine this, simply shut down the circulation system and fill the pond to its appropriate water level. Unplug the pump and leave the pond shut down for at least 12 hours. If the pond's water level drops during that time, allow it to continue drop-

ping. Wherever the water level eventually remains, will be the starting point of a full pond perimeter search. A pinhole or tear in the liner is the most difficult leak to find, but once found, a simple primer and liner patch will remedy the problem.

The good news is that 99 percent of all leaks are not in the pond at all, but rather the low edges of the stream and waterfall area. Since these areas of a water feature are typically built up during construction, the potential for ground settling is much greater. If the ground settles enough over the years and through the seasons, the stream liner may eventually sink and allow water to escape over the edge. To locate a low edge, simply walk along the stream and move the gravel to expose the liner's edge. Once the leak is found, it's very easy to backfill the settled edge with dirt and re-do the gravel edging. If all else fails, contact a water garden professional for assistance.

Mechanical Skimmer – See **Filters**

Nets

Nets are a big help in controlling debris in your pond. The debris net gathers leaves and other materials in your skimmer, while fish nets can be used to wrangle out any large leaves that have fallen onto your pond. Protective netting can also be put over your pond.

Problem	Cause	Remedy
Bubbles in the biological filter	Cracked pipe	Repair pipe
Impeller turns but it won't push water	Vapor lock	Remove pump from water, turn on its side, then reinstall
Pump whining	Possible loss of oil or bad bearing	Check warranty, replace pump
Tripping the breaker	Electrical short	Call your electrician, check electrical line

Oxygenation
See **Winterization**

Pumps and Plumbing

Pumps and plumbing make up the circulatory system of a water feature. Pump and pipe size are extremely important for the aesthetics of a pond, but more importantly, they supply the system with the necessary oxygen levels and keep the water circulating. Most of the larger pumps (1,500 gph or greater) prove to have a three to four year life expectancy. However, some pumps could last eight years and some could last less than one year. Proper pump maintenance and troubleshooting should keep a pump's life going to its full potential. Follow the troubleshooting section above to identify problems and diagnosis you may encounter when dealing with pumps and plumbing in a pond.

Quality of Life
Yours will increase once you get a pond of your own.

Rocks

Rocks don't need to be spic and span in your pond. A little bit of moss and algae can make your pond look more natural. During your spring clean-out, however, power washing your rocks would be beneficial.

Proper pump maintenance and troubleshooting should keep a pump's life going to its full potential.

Spring Clean-outs

Spring clean-outs replenish the water in a pond and allow it to begin a fresh, new season. Since a balanced ecosystem keeps the pond healthy the rest of the year, an annual clean-out gets it off to the right start. Spring algae blooms occur because of excess nutrients and deficient amounts of beneficial bacteria. In a clean-out, the stale pond water is replaced with fresh, clean water that is ready for bacterial colonization. Cleaning a pond in the spring simulates the normal flushing action that stream-fed lakes, streams, and rivers experience during heavy spring rains.

Does every pond need an annual spring clean-out?

Every pond is different, and some ponds do not require an annual clean-out. Ponds larger than 2,000 square feet might only need a clean-out every few years. Larger ponds may never need a complete clean-out because any impurities present are minimal compared to the volume of water in the pond. The larger the pond, the easier it is to maintain (just like a fish tank). You can tell whether the pond needs a spring clean-out by looking at the pond. If it looks the same in March as it did last June, it's probably okay to skip the clean-out.

If you're doing a clean-out, acclimating your fish is very important to their health.

What about ponds in the southern states?

Obviously, ponds located in the warmer climates of the country won't experience a winter quite like those in colder climates. Warm-climate ponds will sustain bacterial life year-round, and may not require a full pond clean-out. However, a partial clean-out is still recommended. Spraying down the filtration media and doing a 20 percent water change annually will prove to be beneficial for the entire system.

10 Steps to a Successful Spring Clean-out

1. **Drain the Pond** – An inexpensive screened pump is sufficient, but don't forget to fill a separate container with pond water for the fish.
2. **Disconnect the Circulation System** – This will allow the water in the plumbing to drain.
3. **Catch the Fish** – Drain the pond to roughly six inches of water in order to catch fish easily and safely.
4. **Remove Debris** – All large debris, such as leaves and twigs, should be removed by hand.
5. **Wash the Pond** – A 1,500psi pressure washer or a high-pressure nozzle on a garden hose is recommended for pond cleaning.
6. **Rinse the Pond** – Rinse the pond from top to bottom with a garden hose while continuing to pump out the dirty water.
7. **Clean the Filters** – Spray down the filtration media until relatively clean and rinse down the actual filter units.
8. **Refill the Pond** – Pull the clean-out pump out and begin refilling the pond.
9. **De-chlorinate the Water** – Most city water contains chlorine and chloramines and should be treated with a de-chlorinator before fish are introduced.
10. **Acclimate the Fish** – A spring clean-out can be stressful to fish, so proper acclimation is suggested to decrease stress and avoid future health problems.

*T*emperature

The minimum water temperature for adding bacteria and feeding your fish 50°F.

UV Lights

Most bulbs need to be replaced every season. After 9-12 months, the efficiency of the bulb may begin to fail. There are two categories of UV lights: sterilizers (high wattage) and clarifiers (low wattage).

*W*ater Quality

Activated carbon has the unique ability to pull dissolved organic carbons from tea-colored water.

Symptom	Problem	Remedy
Brown "tea-colored" Water	Breakdown of organic material (mainly leaves)	Activated carbon
Cloudy Water	Suspended materials	Flocculants
Green Water	Suspended algae	Beneficial bacteria, flocculants, U.V. light, more plants
High Ammonia	Nutrient overload	Ammonia detox solution
High Chlorine or Chloramines	Added during municipal water treatment	Dechlorinator
High Nitrate	Nutrient overload	Beneficial bacteria, plants
High pH	High mineral content (hard water)	pH adjusting or equalizing solution
Low pH	Very soft water easily turned acidic	pH adjusting or equalizing solution
Orange Water	High iron content	Allow time for dissipation, treat water source
Surface Foam	Protein build-up from the pond floor	Organic foam removal solution, physical removal

Winterization

Winterization is not necessary for all ponds. Climate is a big factor when determining whether a pond has a real need for such seasonal maintenance. Debris cleanup from the fall may be inevitable in any part of the country, but only ponds that experience ice-cover over long periods of time will require winterization.

When should pond winterization be done?

Winter preparation should be started after the trees have ceased dropping their leaves in the late fall. Properly winterizing a pond at this time of year will make it easier for an annual clean-out the following spring.

What should be done for ponds with heavy tree cover?

Since a mechanical skimmer filter won't catch all of the surface debris, and not all ponds have a skimmer filter, the use of a net may be necessary to remove the leaves and organics left in the pond during the fall. Debris left to rot in the pond will eventually decompose, producing gases that can be harmful to the fish. Physically removing the leaves and sticks from the pond will make a spring clean-out easier, and may even save the life of a few dormant fish.

Ponds surrounded by thick trees may require more maintenance during the fall, when the trees lose the majority of their leaves. Sometimes a net can be placed over the pond to keep leaves out. Be sure to check the pond's debris net or basket daily during this time of the year to ensure the system functions properly.

What about the plants?

Cutting back plant material in the fall will prevent organic debris from decomposing in the water over the winter. Hardy bog and marginal plants should have all of the dead leaves and foliage trimmed down to 2" above water level, and hardy lily leaves and stems should be cut back, leaving approximately 2-3" at the base of the plant. Tropical plants can be brought inside for winter, or treated as annuals and replaced each season.

A pump that provides at least 2,000 gph can be operated throughout the winter without a problem, as long as it runs continuously.

Can a pond run throughout the entire winter?

Maintenance is usually the determining factor in whether or not a pond owner keeps their pump running in the winter. The primary maintenance responsibility at this time is to make sure there is enough water for the pump(s) to operate properly.

During the winter months, the usual water supply options are not available. Outdoor water spigots and automatic water fill valves should be turned off to prevent pipes from freezing and cracking. Therefore, pond owners who run their systems during the winter will have to find an alternate water source to replenish their pond. Water can be supplied via a hose run from inside the house or by making multiple trips with a five-gallon bucket. Generally speaking, it's not uncommon to have to go out a few times a month during the winter to "top-off" the pond.

Won't the waterfall freeze solid?

Pump size is important when determining a waterfall's ability to operate during the winter. A pump that provides at least 2,000 gph can be operated throughout the winter without a problem, as long as it runs continuously. Moving water will usually keep a hole open in the ice around the waterfalls and in front of the circulation system. However, repeated days in sub-zero temperatures may lead to excessive ice build-up and can cause the system to operate improperly. If the flow of water into the circulation system is unable to keep up with the pump because of ice build-up, it may be necessary to shut the system down. The system can be run again once the ice is melted and normal water flow is restored.

Tip: If the pump is turned off during a heavy freeze, be sure to remove any back-flow obstacles from the circulation system. Other-wise, the remaining water will freeze solid, and although this may not hurt flexible PVC pipe, ice may remain into the spring, preventing the start-up of the pond.

Warning: Slow-Moving Streams

There is nothing more breathtaking than a waterfall covered with ice formations and snow during the winter. You must, however, be careful with ponds that have long or slow-moving streams. In such cases, ice dams can form and divert water over the liner.

Will the filters and pipes crack?

Most good filters are constructed out of rotational-molded polyethylene, and are designed to bow and bend with the freezing and thawing effects of winter. The PVC flex pipe is reinforced and will also not crack unless water is left in the pipe over the winter and allowed to freeze. If you decide to keep the pump running all winter long, there will still be a constant flow of water traveling through the pipe, and the moving water will not freeze. If you decide to turn the system off for the winter, most of the water in the pipe will drain back into the pond when the circulation system is removed.

A heater keeps a hole open for gas exchange, but this alone does not oxygenate the water.

What should be done with the pump once the system is shut down?

Remove the pump from the system and store it in a frost-free location, ideally submerged in a bucket of water. The water around the pump housing will prevent the seals on the pump from drying and cracking. Since most submersible pumps are oil-filled, it is not suggested to let the freeze solid.

Tip: To extend the life of the pump, it is suggested to clear the impeller shaft free of any debris before winter storage. It is also beneficial to spin the impeller a couple of turns by hand before turning it on in the spring. This will prevent any corrosion or debris from seizing the impeller and interrupting proper pump function.

What about the filter?

When preparing the pond for winter, remove the filtration media and rinse it down. It is recommended to store any such media in a frost-free location like a garage or shed. If left over the winter, all of the filtration media may freeze into a solid block, causing unnecessary delays during the spring clean-out.

What about the fish? Will they be okay?

Ornamental fish will do just fine in two feet of water, as long as some form of oxygenation is provided, and a hole is kept in the ice to allow the escape of harmful gases. It's recommended to place the waterfall pump in a basket, bucket, or pump sock and surround the intake of the pump with stones to prevent clogging. Place the pump on the second or third shelf of the pond so the surface water is broken by the aeration. The agitation from the pump will prevent freezing and provide oxygen.

Another option is to use a floating heater in combination with a small submersible pump (at least 150 gph). You can place the small re-circulating pump on the first shelf of the pond, bubbling at least one inch above the surface. Floating heaters are the most common method of keeping a hole open in the ice. Unfortunately they won't provide oxygen for the fish, and some can be expensive to operate. Do not confuse a floating pond de-icer with a water heater. A pond de-icer won't heat the water; it will simply keep a small hole open in the ice. Be sure to place the heater away from re-circulating water to avoid moving the heated water.

The Bottom Line

The bottom line for winterization is maintenance. Roughly 70 percent of pond owners in the colder climates decide to shut down their system because they don't enjoy tending to their water garden during the bitter months of the winter. The aesthetic rewards of the "winter pond" are absolutely worthwhile, so by all means, don't be afraid to keep the system running as long as possible. Shutting down a pond during winter is also an option. Just be sure you take precautionary measures to preserve fish, plant, and pump life.

X, Y, and Z

Now that you know your Pond A, B, C's … you can't wait to see what spring will bring.

The aesthetic rewards of the "winter pond" are absolutely worthwhile, so keep the system running as long as possible.

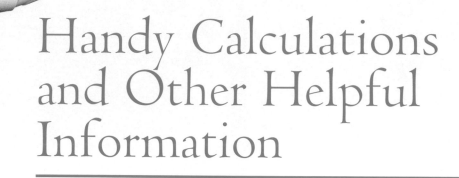

Handy Calculations and Other Helpful Information

Hardiness Zone Map

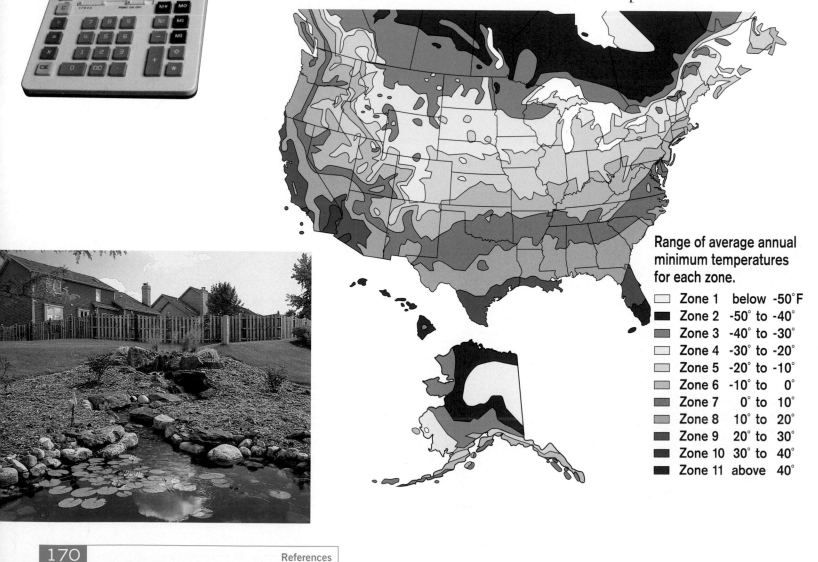

Range of average annual minimum temperatures for each zone.

Zone 1	below	-50°F
Zone 2	-50° to	-40°
Zone 3	-40° to	-30°
Zone 4	-30° to	-20°
Zone 5	-20° to	-10°
Zone 6	-10° to	0°
Zone 7	0° to	10°
Zone 8	10° to	20°
Zone 9	20° to	30°
Zone 10	30° to	40°
Zone 11	above	40°

Information Resources

www.aquascapedesigns.com
www.nawgs.com
www.nurserypro.com
www.pondandgarden.com

Plants for Water Gardens; By Helen Nash and Steve Stroupe. Sterling Publishing, New York, NY
Water Gardening: Water Lilies and Lotuses; By Perry D. Slocum, Peter Robinson, and Frances Perry. Timber Press, Portland, OR

Charts and Conversions

- **Approximate Gallons of Water in a Pond**
  Irregular Pond: average length x average width x average depth x 7.48 = total gallons in pond
  Circular Pond: πr^2 x average depth x 7.48 = total gallons in pond

- **Approximate Gallons of Water in a Stream**
  Length x Width x .25 x 7.48 = Gallons in a stream

- **Electrical Consumption**
  Amps x Volts ÷ 1000 x .10 (avg. kw per hour) x 24 hrs x 30.4 days = Monthly cost
- Conversions to help with electrical calculations:
  Watts = volts x amps
  Amps = watts ÷ volts

- **Calcualtion for Quantity of Fish**
  1" of fish per 1 sq. ft. of pond surface area

Calculating Liner Size

- 2 x pond depth + Maximum Pond Length = Liner Length
- 2 x pond depth + Maximum Pond Width = Liner Width

Example: For an 11' x 16' pond that is 2-feet deep, you would need a 15' x 20' liner.
(2 x 2' + 11' = 15') x (2 x 2' + 16' = 20') = liner size

Rock and Gravel Calculations

Boulders:
- In the Pond
  - Formula: Length in feet x width in feet / 40.
  - Example: 11 x 16 = 176 / 40 = 4.4. Round up to 4 ½ or 5 tons to be safe.
  - Tip: For a more natural look, use an assortment of sizes. Aquascape recommends a mixture of 6 to 12" and 12 to 18" granite boulders. For a really great effect, you can include about a ½ ton of 18 to 36" boulders to set into the edge of the pond. These make great sitting stones for feeding your fish.
- In the Stream
  - Formula: 1 ½ tons of boulders for every 10' of stream length.
  - Example: The stream that leads from your waterfall to your pond is 20' long, you would need 3 tons of boulders.
  - Tip: For a great assortment of sizes, use a 1:2:1 ratio of 6 to 12", 12 to 18", and 18-24" boulders. The larger stones will be used to naturalize the edge of the stream.
- For the Waterfall
  - Formula: Small Waterfall = 1 ton of assorted boulders, Medium Waterfall = 1 ½ tons of assorted boulders, Large Waterfall = 2 to 3 tons of assorted boulders.
  - Example: Your pond has a medium waterfall, so you'll need 1 ½ tons of boulders.
  - Tip: Framing the waterfall with larger boulders will help create a natural-looking cascade of water.

Gravel:
- In the Pond
  - Formula: 30% of the total quantity of pond boulders.
  - Example: Your pond contains 4.4 tons of boulders, so you would need 1.32 tons of gravel.
  - Tip: Ask your rock yard for a mixture of assorted sizes ranging from ½ to 3" gravel. This serves a number of purposes, including prevention of compaction and flexibility of filling gaps in the larger rocks.
- In the Stream
  - Formula: 30% of the total quantity of stream boulders.
  - Example: Your stream contains 3 tons of boulders, so you would need .9 tons of gravel.
  - Tip: Ask your rock yard for a mixture of assorted sizes ranging from ½ to 3" gravel. This serves a number of purposes, including prevention of compaction and flexibility of filling gaps in the larger rocks.

Index

Index

Index

The North American Water Garden Society & Aquascape Lifestyles Magazine
WE'RE ALL ABOUT THE HOBBY!

NAWGS is an organization of pond lovers dedicated to the enjoyment, education, promotion, and protection of the water garden hobby.

N.A.W.G.S.™
North American Water Garden Society

JOIN!

NAWGS Trial Membership:
Test the Water – ONLY $35! ($49.95 value)
Includes a 1-year subscription to *Aquascape Lifestyles* magazine!

Unite with Like-Minded Lovers of Water Gardening!
Local gatherings and a continent-wide network are waiting for you!

Make Waves!
Ride the wave of Pond Tour North America – water gardening's premiere showcase event, coming to a location near you.

Shape the Future!
NAWGS raises up a whole new generation of kids with a heart for the environment through Ponds for Kids.

Immerse Yourself in a Significant Way!
NAWGS supports research that protects our hobby, like a $50,000 gift to the University of Georgia for koi herpes virus research – the largest sum raised so far. We seek to be the go-to resource for legislators.

FREE! to you with your NAWGS Membership

SUBSCRIBE!

Support NAWGS by subscribing to *Aquascape Lifestyles* magazine

1 Year Subscription: $21.97
2 Years Only $34.97 BEST DEAL

Discover *Aquascape Lifestyles* magazine… a full-color, glossy masterpiece completely devoted to you – the water garden lover.

Be inspired – *Aquascape Lifestyles* is packed cover-to-cover with expert secrets, amazing photos, and the hottest trends in the water garden world, all guaranteed to arouse your imagination!

Get educated – Each and every issue is filled to the max with info that will make you the expert: tips on having the most gorgeous pond in town, maintaining your water garden's health and well-being, and mastering the ins and outs of pond-keeping.

Subscribe to *Aquascape Lifestyles* or
Join NAWGS online: www.nawgs.org
Call Toll Free: 1.877.206.7035 or use Mail-in card!

Join the North American Water Garden Society

NAWGS is an organization of pond lovers dedicated to the enjoyment, education, promotion & protection of the water gardening hobby.

FREE! to you with your NAWGS Membership

Application for Membership:

Name _____

Address _____

City _____ State/Province _____

Zip/Postal Code _____ Country _____

E-mail _____

Test the Water! Join NAWGS!
☐ 1-year Trial Membership $35.00

Subscribe to Aquascape Lifestyles
☐ 1-Year $21.97
☐ 2-Years $34.97 Best Deal!

Allow 6-8 weeks for delivery. U.S. funds only.

☐ Check #_____ ☐ Credit Card ☐ Bill Me

Visa/Master Card # _____ Exp. Date _____

Card Holder's Signature _____

Return this form via mail *(checks made payable to North American Water Garden Society)* **to:**

P.O. Box 3697 • St. Charles, IL 60174-9088
or Fax form with credit card info to: 630.659.2100
or Call with credit card info: 877.206.7035

For more information visit www.nawgs.org
KEYCODE: BEPB35

BUSINESS REPLY MAIL
FIRST-CLASS MAIL   PERMIT NO. X   ST. CHARLES, IL

POSTAGE WILL BE PAID BY ADDRESSEE

NORTH AMERICAN WATER GARDEN SOCIETY
PO BOX 3697
ST CHARLES, IL 60174-9088